John Price

Remarks on the Study of Languages, and Hints on Comparative Translation

And Philological Construing

John Price

Remarks on the Study of Languages, and Hints on Comparative Translation
And Philological Construing

ISBN/EAN: 9783337241834

Printed in Europe, USA, Canada, Australia, Japan

Cover: Foto ©Thomas Meinert / pixelio.de

More available books at **www.hansebooks.com**

REMARKS

ON THE

STUDY OF LANGUAGES,

AND HINTS ON

COMPARATIVE TRANSLATION

AND

PHILOLOGICAL CONSTRUING.

FOURTH EDITION.

RE-PRINTED FROM "*OLD PRICE'S REMAINS*," WITH OTHER ARTICLES,
AND AN INTRODUCTION.

By J. PRICE, M.A.,

FORMERLY SCHOLAR OF ST. JOHN'S, CAMBRIDGE;
A MASTER OF SHREWSBURY SCHOOL, AND OF THE BRISTOL COLLEGE.

LONDON:
LONGMANS & CO.
LIVERPOOL: ADAM HOLDEN, CHURCH STREET.
1869.

Price 2s. 6d.

DEDICATED

TO

YOUNG SHREWSBURY,

FROM ADMIRATION OF THE STYLE IN WHICH THEY MAINTAIN
THE UNPARALLELED RENOWN

OF

OLD SHREWSBURY.

PREFACE TO THE FOURTH EDITION.

THE Author must, without any excuses, beg indulgence for the imperfections in this edition of a work which, *at length,* appears *in a more readable form,* according to the suggestion (in 1857) of an eminent reader whose name appears elsewhere, and whose good opinion was deservedly valued. The various critical and other articles, added to illustrate or enliven the STUDY OF LANGUAGES, are so ill *arranged,* that the " *etc.*" at the head of page 111 might as well have appeared on *several* previous pages. Some *headings* are also needlessly repeated. None of these errata, however, are due to the Printer, whose faults do not seem worth mentioning.

38, WATERGATE STREET, CHESTER.
March 20th, 1869.

INTRODUCTION.

ONE of the most striking facts connected with the defective state of our "Higher Education" is, that a considerable amount of what is propounded on the subject (in Parliament and elsewhere) exhibits a remarkable want of intelligence, in the speakers and writers, respecting *the educational process itself.* This special form of ignorance may perhaps be said both to stand at the head and to lie at the root of the many defects they are labouring to amend; and is the less curable because it prevails so generally amongst the educated, a class to whom the nation naturally looks for suggestions of reform. In vain will it look, where the class in question, Educational Reformers, rest content with a wholesale examination of schools, systems, and books, rather than try to ascertain, in detail, how they were taught themselves—what it was that brought them so far, and why no farther. That this task is difficult, and only to a limited extent possible, may well be conceded. But any little discovery of the steps in so complicated a "latens processus" is of such high practical value, that it is well worth while to retrace our steps, à teneris unguibus, in search of the several doors that were opened, the avenues that did *not* turn out culs de sac, the habits that proved fruitful in results, &c.; and, on the contrary, the rubbish or boards that closed up other doors and passages, the practices and attempts that ended in barrenness, &c.

Another source of information touching these intellectual arcana is open to those who have the opportunity of experimenting, with their own acquired stores, upon the carte blanche (*ou bien, souillée*) of other minds. And it must be allowed, that our theoretical reformers labour under serious disadvantages, if they never attempted, for themselves personally, the practical work of teaching ; though even this drawback will hardly suffice to account for the supernatural quantity of nonsense spoken and written, on grand occasions. One is reminded of Lyell's suggestion as to the probable views of a Gnome—a subterranean sprite—concerning geological changes, in order to illustrate the opposite prejudices arising from our *peculiar* position as denizens of the surface! And again, even in the privileged class of teachers, those whose time is devoted exclusively to one branch, or to pupils of one age, or of the same sex, must necessarily find that, with a limited sphere, their opportunities of observation are also circumscribed. " Ut de me loquar, quoniam id ætati nostræ conceditur," I consider that more than 40 years spent in instructing pupils of both sexes, of the greatest variety of ages, singly and in classes, " *de rebus omnibus et quibusdam aliis,*" gives me such a vantage ground that those who have had " no such chance " might perhaps expect me to judge their faux pas more charitably! *And so I should,* if *the poor things were subpœna'd :* on the contrary, they *volunteer* their crudities, and expect us to listen with patience, if not to thank them, " capite obstipo."

I have noticed, in page 9, the probable influence of the bare grammar-school training of the olden time upon many of our by-gone intellectual giants ; but, since that was written, (1850) I think I have learnt somewhat more of the secret *causes* of that "mighty magic." Archbishop Whately remarks, that the process of reasoning never goes beyond an act analogous to restoring a book found on the floor to its own place in the library ; or (conversely) going to the right spot on the shelf to reach a required book. The highest and most abstruse investigations of Newton, on his majestic march from the known to the unknown, are (according to that lucid writer) nothing more than a grand concatenation of progressive steps, every one of which can be reduced to that simple type of accurate recognition and collocation.

Now, if this be the case, it is clear that all employments leading to the habit of referring, easily and rapidly, *any* item, of *any* kind whatever, to its assigned locale in *any* systematic arrangement whatever, must have a tendency to improve the mind in the practice of reasoning, since the *mental procedure is* always exactly the same, however diverse the subjects with which it has to deal. This gives an educational value to *systematic* Botany, Zoology, &c., in addition to their obvious effect in quickening the powers of observation and comparison. All experience, however, shows that the early inculcation of a classified nomenclature of such objects often serves to render the whole subject permanently distasteful; and that it answers better to defer that part of tuition till the pupils, having acquired an interest in the *individual* plants, animals, &c., are glad of the scientific arrangement and "hard *names*," as an indispensable help to their own thoughts and conversation about the *things*. It is time enough to "endorse" when they have acquired "bundles of ideas" to write on. And I believe, if we ransacked the whole range of existing or possible lessons for *beginners,* we should not find *one* of such obvious practical utility in habituating the mind to the process thus illustrated by Whately, as the old-fashioned, humdrum, invariable, and *inevitable* practice of making children repeat Verbs by rote, till they can, at a glance, *tell* the class, conjugation, voice, mood, tense, number, and person, of any one they meet with in reading; or, when writing exercises, *choose* the right person, number, tense, &c., corresponding to the English verb they are translating.   If Whately be right, children so employed are, unconsciously to themselves, daily improving in a practice calculated, *above any other as yet within their reach,* to facilitate the progress by which *alone* the highest problems of science have been, step by step, conducted; the process also, be it remembered, by which alone *right* conclusions can be drawn *with certainty* in the most ordinary transactions of domestic life, even to the making of rice pudding or onion sauce— [pet questions in *applied* Botany.]

Our author, in his Logic, (Book I., sec. 4, p. 20, 9th edition, 8vo,) says, " Now to remind one, on each occasion, that so " and so is referable to such and such a class, and that the " class which happens to be before us comprehends such and " such things—this is precisely all that is ever accomplished " by Reasoning." I cannot *find* the previous illustration from the Librarian's task, either in the Logic, or " Easy Lessons in Reasoning" (the drier and harder of the two!)—mais c'est bien lui; and whether it be his own, or the work of a commentator—whether all my readers *precisely* agree with it or not, is of no consequence to my purpose.   I wish to impress my own conviction that, at the age when children usually learn the inflexions in the Latin and Greek accidence, they are imperceptibly acquiring a power of correct classification, available for logical purposes, whilst express lessons in the "Art of Reasoning" would be premature and repulsive.

I am perfectly sure that any little girl who has got so far in Greek grammar as to be expert in the Paradigms, and in the drawing of a Greek tree, not only *can* reason, but (from the sheer habit of accurate and rapid classification,) *cannot help* reasoning with more readiness, and correctness, than that same child could after any other preparation. I should certainly recommend further progress in the language, where time and circumstances permit. But, let those who go so far and *no* further, instead of regretting mis-spent time, "thank God and take courage"—they have gained *immensely*, even by that little investment; tho' it is of course set at nought by that large (and, it is to be feared, influential) class who can see no inducement to learn Greek besides the acquisition of that language, and an acquaintance with its literature. I confine *these* remarks to Greek, because, though the verbs in any language furnish the same *kind* of discipline, classification becomes much ampler and more refined, owing to the fuller development of that part of speech, where there are two widely different classes (in ω and μι) with a middle voice, an optative mood, several tenses, and a dual number, all unknown to Latin; and where the established "formation of tenses" serves at any rate, even where most fanciful, as a good memorial assistance to simplify the comprehension of the vast and admirable framework.

It is sufficiently obvious that, to those who proceed, as is highly desirable, beyond the accidence of either language, the perpetual reference to both Dictionary and Grammar, which is indispensable to arrive *honestly* at the sense of the author, and the application, in parsing, of *classified* syntax rules, (all in short that is included in the "study of classics") must further improve the mind in the very same (logical) direction. In fact, the "disciplinal" as well as the literary element in *such* a course is fully admitted by those who never dream that the mere inflexions of nouns, adjectives, and verbs, can furnish anything beyond a parrot-like gabble, beneficial to the *memory alone.* But we next come to a totally distinct department, still less suspected of yielding any intellectual improvement outside the range of "Reminiscor *obliviscor*, memini, recordor." I mean the dry study of Prosody—the laws of "feet" and metre ; the antidote to that terrible calamity, " a false quantity," such as Edmund Burke's " vectĭgal !" or the Eton traditional " Descĕndē cælo, et dĭc agē tibīa Regīnā longum Calliōpe mēlos."

I have in p. 54, under "Nonsense Verses," discussed the merits of that despised branch of education, considered as a *classical* necessity. But to the point *now* in hand, viz., the preparation of the mind for a habit of right reasoning, it need only be remarked that, with Prosody, the pupil commences a new classification, not only of inflected words, as nouns and verbs, but of the *whole language,* to the smallest particle; and that too upon a *totally different ground* of adjustment, being now guided by the "time" or "quantity" of the syllables, considered as quavers and semiquavers, irrespective of their meaning; the Gradus and Jani Ars poetica, with scanning and proving, now taking place of the Dictionary and Grammar, with construing and parsing. And here the selections or rejections (pro re natâ), the arrangements and re-arrangements, the φροντιδες and δευτεραι φροντιδες, are all directed by considerations so strictly *logical*, (in Whately's sense) that a greater educational blunder could not well be made, than by supposing a student who had acquired the ("mere mechanical"!) art of making *nonsense* Elegiacs must have simply wasted so much time, unless he proceed to earn a place in the Musæ Etonenses or Sabrinæ Corolla. On the contrary, he has been going through a course of mental gymnastics which, (unless perchance he "take leave of his senses" and cease, viciously, to be a reasoning being,) *can not fail* to exercise a beneficial influence as long as he lives. Such influence will of course be denied by that school of Philosophers who consider each branch of education *merely* as a means to one *particular* end, instead of viewing every one of them as being, far *more* truly, so many various means to one great *general* end, viz., "the strengthening and developing, by artificial means, of the natural resources of the human intellect."

I gladly accept this, as *one* definition of education, from an article in the March number, 1869, of the MUSEUM (Nelson & Sons, London), by my old pupil, David Ker ; who, having quitted the Isis (I need not say with what credit), is, I venture to guess, *thawing* the Neva, on the very lowest hypothesis of applied caloric, at St. Petersburg, whence he dates an article that may call in question the alleged difficulty of "putting old heads on young shoulders." His subject, "UNCONSCIOUS EDUCATION," is indeed a wide and suggestive one, extending far beyond the professed sphere of these pages. But his idea *includes* mine most strictly and strikingly ; besides which, the essay commends itself to me by its moral inculcations, falling in with a favourite old maxim of my own, that the *successful* candidate may very often not benefit near so much by the result of a competitive examination, as *many others* who have been induced by it to raise themselves *far more than he has*, above the previous status in quo. And I am sure my assertion in p. 9, that the direct benefit of classics is surpassed by the indirect, &c., would be found, if we possessed a gauge for such measurements, equally true of every study that fairly taxes the industry and talent of the learner. Now I contend that these are the *most* evergreen laurels—these are the "distinctions" which *do* distinguish a man from his fellows, when University honors are forgotten, or where they were never heard of; this indefeasible treasure maintains both income and position for "that moral centaur, man and wife," (cum vel sine pertinentibus) after a barbarous (and, thanks to R. P., now moribund) statute has deprived the single gentleman of his well-earned fellowship, as a penalty on the wisest act of his life! Hæ denique sunt "ea viatica, quæ cum naufrago enatent."

But, in this long and versatile career of tuition, it would be strange indeed if none of the *hindrances* to our noble craft had made themselves visible, *en passant*, to the (naked or assisted) mind's eye, as well as the aids and facilities. Would that I could say my own failures had not contributed an ample contingent to this catalogue; not that the sense of these at all augments my "common patience" with those prim Seers, who presume to dictate to the whole educational world, without having had the honour of even *blundering* in our honourable profession. But, *a verbatim Report is their best flagellation.*

I was once occupied, very earnestly (it may yet serve as a suggestion to better managers,) in making a minute collection of school-boys' mistakes, *vivâ voce* and written, with a view to arranging them under their several heads—Languages, Geography, Natural History, &c., and endeavouring to trace them to their causes, in the minds of the taught or in the method and books of the teacher.   The regret expressed at their loss (by fire ? or three removes ?) on the part of an esteemed friend (Ω), went to my heart, for I had never before felt *sure* of their statistical value.   It was a bitter "drop in the sea "—of troubles.

Our present business, however, is rather with errors in the teacher than the taught.

It is, first of all, a grand mistake to make any study, at the outset, more uninteresting than it need be, for want of devising ways and means to enliven it.   I once heard a very litte girl say, "Whenever we have to learn a new thing with Papa, he always begins it with us *in a joke !*" And I have always thought that, *so far at least*, that Parent had hit upon the right course in elementary training. There can be no doubt that, for some years past, " Wit and Humour," dry and *sundry*, has occupied an excessive share in the Literature of this country ; especially since the comic quill and pencil have been subsidized by *rival-factions*, as a political necessity, till the pair of Jocular Serials in each window remind one of village lads grinning through horse collars for a prize !   But that is no reason why our youngsters and youngstresses should not, now and then, and within bounds, be "carried past the wearisome bitterness of their learning," by the judicious admixture of a little spice of merriment, which is apt to lighten the heart of the teacher too.   That dull chapter on cases and their signs, (Eton gr. pp. 2 and 3,) has been greatly enlivened " in my poor judgment" (Hooker), ever since "O! Magister" presented itself to me as the natural effect of a smart caneing from the said "master" who, after listening æquo animo to the *moderate* amount of respect in the previous "doctrina magistri," and so forth, may well be supposed to have lost *all* patience, when the young varlet dared to affirm, to his face, that "he *loved* the master!!" ὠ τυμπανα και κυφωνες ! We may safely pronounce a dull method to be a fault in the educator.

Another decided pest to children and parents is the needless change of books.   As to *Grammars,* it must be a *far* better than the world has yet seen, (1869,) that *ought* to displace* *entirely* almost any one of the common school grammars a pupil may *happen to be accustomed to.*   A 'line drawn through the words "Substantive," "Potential," "Can," "Could," &c., &c., and a few other slight MS. changes, together with some brief directions given in "Helps to construing" (p. 48) will, *with intelligent teaching,* soon convert an old Eton brown Bess into a tolerable breech-loading rifle, far more practically useful than a totally new "arm" which the poor children can only hope to *begin* to understand when they shall have (if possible) so far recovered the shock of being thrown back by a violent change, as to be tolerable scholars, and therefore, by that time, in a measure independent of books, good or bad.   It is a *very curious fact* that, the more decidedly these smashing novelties improve *some* of the defects of our predecessors, the more decidedly do they ruin (by ignoring ?) *many* of their excellencies ! So that, when I see the brilliant attempts

* *A better grammar, used as a book of reference, may effect,* quietly, *far more good,* at a *radical reform* self-defeated by *radical errors*, I am constrained to exclaim, in all sincerity, with the old French officer witnessing the gallant but disastrous cavalry charge at Balaclava:—" C'est magnifique! mais *ce n'est pas la guerre."* But this is a subject on which I would fain speak more specifically elsewhere.

Since want of interest in the subject matter is the greatest hindrance to the student in any branch of learning, it seems unwise to overlook any means by which its dryness, real or imaginary, may be removed or alleviated. And, fortunately for teachers, the existence of a bond of connexion between even the most dissimilar departments of knowledge, greatly facilitates such measures of relief. It is notorious that those who have a special aptitude for arithmetic, and the rest of mathematics, are often afflicted with a *distaste* (often mistaken for incapacity) for the study of language. Now, there are many ways of introducing numerical considerations in teaching classics, which may help these juvenile Unilaterals out of what they are pleased to consider " their difficulty." Many linguistic facts are best learnt, even in ordinary cases, by the pupil's own arrangement of them, on a statistical plan, in tables and in columns, to refresh the arithmetical mind. Some, again, admit of being stated in the form of a proportion; *e.g.*, Adjective : Noun : : Adverb : Verb, which can not choose but remind the little accountants of their darling Rule of Three! Then, when it comes to versification, whence all the nine Muses might be supposed to have expelled Bonnycastle & Co. with one pitch-fork, the numeral element in the question of feet and half-feet, consisting of 1, 2, or 3 syllables, enters jure suo as an essential part of the study.

Besides which, a little consideration will enable the teacher to imbue the process of scanning with an almost Algebraic tinge. Having ascertained the maximum and minimum of a hexameter to be 17 and 13 syllables respectively, and observed that the lines always end with a dactyl and spondee, our young Parnassian Excelsior will feel justified in setting aside the last 5 syllables, and the first (long in any wise), as "known quantities" or "given." Besides which, as fast as each of the 4 remaining feet is ascertained, the next syllable *becomes* a known quantity. Thus, 9 syllables being disposed of by mere observation, there remain only from 4 to 8 requiring the trouble of further investigation. Nay, further, if, after ascertaining 2 out of the 4 unknown feet, Tyro should descry, by "simple inspection," that 4 syllables remain, after striking off the last 5 (which should be done with a pencil at the outset, to assist the eye), these 4 must needs be *all long*—2 spondees. In which case the virtually unknown are reduced to 4 at the most, and may be only 2. I recommend the scanning of lines from *these* data, and the determination of the length of syllables by *common sense*, previous to "technical proving" by the rules of Prosody; always to try for dactyls, till you are stopped by a diphthong, or two consonants, (which *actually* lengthen the syllable,) being a very safe general rule.

More need not be said; though there are other ways of so introducing the manufacture of longs and shorts to the embryo VATES, that it *sha'nt* be dry.

It might almost be said that, *à fortiori*, other subjects can be interwoven with classics besides arithmetic, which we have just seen acting the "Tutor's Assistant" under difficulties. No sooner have the class learnt, (as is quite

necessary before other *Passive* Verbs,) "Esse to be," than
they should be told—1st, as Joiners, that it is like a ma-
hogany chair with a rush bottom and deal legs, concocted
out of several broken ones ; and—2nd, as Geologists, that it
is a conglomerate, where worn fragments of other verbs are
consolidated into a very useful word-building material, by
a paste of more recent formation. I have a diagram of fero—
tuli—latum, &c., as a mass of rock with the boulders and
matrix variously coloured, to assist this analogy. Zoology
and Botany find themselves very closely imitated,
where portions of verbs drop off, as it were, and set up
for themselves, giving birth to tenses of their own ; as
esurio (from esurus) πολεμησειω (from πολεμησω) τεθνηκω
(from τεθνηκα) ; a process forcibly recalling the "gemmi-
parous reproduction" of Zoophytes, which is, in turn, the
counterpart of a vegetable process, familiar to us in the
cloves of Garlic and the axillary bulbs of the Tiger Lily.

It is a very serious loss, when any *second* language the
children happen to know is not constantly referred to in
the way of comparison with the dead ones. A valued
and kind friend will remember how I regretted her *dropping
the use of Portuguese* in the family, on their arrival from
South America, (*instead of making me, the tutor, learn that
same !*)

Ambiguities are so important a subject, regarding both
the choice of synonyms and the detection of fallacies, that
any help to the study should be thankfully accepted. And,
though a *habit of punning* may, when it runs rampant, become *almost actionable as a nuisance,* yet I have not hesi-
tated to commend the Pun, even in its most atrocious form,
as a philological auxiliary in the study of language, the in-

tolerant and indiscriminate suppression of which I therefore condemn, as an educational misdemeanour. It just occurs to me, that you need not trouble your neighbour with *all* those that develop themselves " in your sleeve." Your *silent* punster may be one of the very best ! But, if you *cannot* either make or apprehend the puns in any given language, believe me you are but imperfectly acquainted with the *niceties* of that language.

There be some severe arbiters, no doubt, who would reject, as hybrids, all puns involving a " cross " between two different languages. But—don't tell *me* that the very best kind of German Barm is not Barmherzigkeit; or that, in that fest-und-grund-bewurzelt country, any sort of Potatoe can compete with die Wohlthäter. If you do, λιθον ἐψεις.

In a world of distraction and bustle, like ours, it is mere cruelty to let children expect the absence of all noise and disturbance when they are at work, except *as an occasional luxury.* The complaint, " Please sir, Sam Brittain is shaking the table," was promptly met by my worthy old master, T. Halton, with " Pooh, man, you must learn to write on the pummel of the saddle, at full trot;" a reply which opened my eyes, in *every* sense! Some years afterwards, as the privileged tutor to Dr. Jas. Cowles Prichard's children, I used to see that genuine Philosopher hard at work (probably on THE PHYSICAL HISTORY OF MAN) in a study where the weans, *at highest romps,* had free ingress and egress—another great lesson on the power of abstraction under difficulties which all should *aim* at. By the way, I suspect Cæsar's habit of doing two things at a time, (*not* four, as we used to fancy when reading of it in Valpy's Delectus!) depended upon a sort of *rhythmical* attention to each, which kept them from actually clashing. But this by the way ; it is pretty well to do *one* thing at a time, and do it properly.

It is a serious mistake to expect from young persons the impossibility of retaining all they ought to learn from oral teaching, *without making notes of their own.* A sixpenny "alphabet ledger," (much used in Liverpool offices,) is a *great* help, especially if the first use made of it be to enter a series of headings, such as—article, conjunction, derivatives, ellipsis, &c., the sight of which serve as a daily incentive to fill up blank spaces. When visiting Manchester Museum, about 1828, I was very much struck with their plan for filling the cases. Though the Entomological room was as yet nearly devoid of specimens, there was a pin, a cork, and a name set up already for *every known insect*, only waiting for the contributions of public spirited collectors. I felt sure that, *with such a broad hint*, their desiderata would shortly be supplied.

The most fatal mistake of all is to omit making a pupil, as early as possible, *master some one thing absolutely, in all its bearings ;* not so much for its own sake, as because that *one* conquered subject, be it ever so simple, will serve ever after as a standard of comparison for the *amount* of victory obtained over other subjects. It is for want of such a test that some adults, having grown up with only a *partial* mastery over each successive step, never learn what it is *really* to know *any* thing ; and thus sometimes even mistake for universal *knowledge* that which is not far removed from the *opposite* condition.

The whole principle involved in this may be seen, on paper, in the hackneyed maxim, " You must learn this as perfect as A, B, C." And in fact, an *accurate* acquaintance with the powers and true relations of the letters of the English Alphabet is so *very* rare an accomplishment, that there is no wonder if all *beyond* that is enveloped in much obscurity, though the bewildered students may have actually learnt the whole cycle of sciences *about* as thoroughly as *their* A, B, C.

With regard to the Higher Education of Women, I am bound to say that, as the writer of some aspirations in the following pages nearly 20 years ago, I am thankful for even that measure of attention which *is*, at last, bestowed on the subject, as an earnest of better things. The Cambridge testimony as to the ability evidenced by Girls is *most satisfactory;* and I am happy to add as the result of my own experience that I have always found their progress in Classics and Mathematics *truly encouraging*, though the amount of time they are allowed to bestow on such subjects is, compared with Boys, *absurdly* small. Let them gladly avail themselves of such opportunities as may be afforded for acquiring *solid* instruction and *elevating* tastes, to counteract *a strong tide of the opposite tendencies.* They will easily refute the notion of that wicked wight who drew a conclusion so unfavourable to the softer sex, from that simple expression in Scott's Marmion, "Ho! shoot not, 'tis a Boy."

I feel sure of patient attention to the following Remarks at the hands of my worthy fellow laborers in the noble work of *Education*. We are not an idle or pampered class at any rate; and, if the Public will not allow us to do them all the good we wish, we can say with Cyrus—*ἰόντων, εἰδότες ὅτι κακίους εἰσὶ περὶ ἡμᾶς ἢ ἡμεῖς περὶ ἐκείνους.*

PREFATORY LETTER,

ADDRESSED, WITH ED. 2, 1850, TO

THE REV. B. H. KENNEDY, D.D.,

HEAD MASTER OF SHREWSBURY SCHOOL.

MY DEAR KENNEDY,

As this little work has been undertaken at your request, I must inflict upon you the perusal of a few extra lines, by way of Preface.

You may perhaps remember that, in our younger days, I used to advise those who meditated throwing themselves upon the British Public, to practise first upon a set of spiked railings, in order to get accustomed to the consequences. I have not myself gone through this preliminary training; and yet you have inveigled me into the experiment in one of its most alarming forms, viz. as an Author! How the said little work will fare amongst the said great Public remains to be proved: but the decided testimony I have received from yourself and Dr. LATHAM, with several others eminently qualified to judge of my plan for translating, would console me under the coldest reception, or the roughest handling.

It is the conviction that this plan embodies an important part of that which was most peculiarly "BUTLERIAN" in Shrewsbury scholarship, that induces me to press its adoption, as far as practicable, in Public as well as Private Tuition. I *know* that you

and I were, *virtually*, taught on this system ; though *we*, poor
fellows, had to squeeze our translations into a single line, and
were never indulged with a drop of "blue ink." And I do hope I
have hit upon a device for inculcating more cogently, and for
practising more definitely and *corrigibly*, that kind of vivid rendering which THE Doctor, by a rare art, above all rules or
machinery, perhaps peculiar to himself, used to infuse into his
Pupils, and elicit from them, at will.

Should I be so fortunate, even with the aid of technicalities,
as to succeed at all in keeping this up, and bringing anything *like*
Butlerian philology, more within the reach of classical students
generally, I believe I should render an important service to education. You will see that my aim goes far beyond the mere
production of Translations, however excellent. The principles I
have laid down will, if worked closely and thoughtfully even with
English translations only, bring one into inevitable collision with
a host of collateral phenomena, both on a great and small scale :
if pursued still higher with other modern tongues, it will carry
one up into the "limiting ratios," as it were, of Philological research, and suggest many a "differential" problem, requiring for
its solution the knowledge of a wider range of languages. So
that I feel convinced at every turn, that I am but furnishing hints
for some abler hand to develope a more powerful calculus for
investigating the laws of thought and speech.

I am sure you lament with me the little justice usually done
to Female Education in its higher departments. Women are
very rarely taught Latin at all, though they require the *indirect*
benefits of it (see page 8), quite as much, and for the same reasons
as any of us ; and, when they learn modern languages, it is I fear
much oftener as a superficial accomplishment, than for solid
intellectual improvement. If the power of making "Comparative

Translations" *from* and *into* French, German, or Italian, were substituted respectively for the *average* School proficiency in those languages, would not Old Shrewsbury, who did so much for "us lads," begin to claim, in turn, the gratitude of the future wives and mothers of England? Bear with my fondness for a pet invention, when I say it would form a new era in their educational history, even if all the French that *is* learnt were *thus* learnt. If you have *The Philosophy of Arithmetic*, by JOHN WALKER, of Dublin, [and if not, why not?] see his title-page and dedication for a principle or two.

But I must not weary you: since the days when you and I learnt our lessons *together*, how many lessons have we had to learn *apart;* how many mercies received: our trials, our disappointments, perhaps amongst the choicest! Above all, we have, I trust, alike entered the School of the BEST of MASTERS, our LORD JESUS CHRIST; and therefore, though separated by distance, are striving together, and by degrees *learning*, to do all things, even in these professional matters, to His praise and glory. That we may do so more and more,—that we may "thank GOD, and take courage,"—is, my dear KENNEDY, the heart's desire and prayer of,

Yours very truly,

JOHN PRICE.

BIRKENHEAD, *June* 7, 1850.

ON THE STUDY. OF LANGUAGES.

IT is a common maxim with the English, that " one ought to learn French *as the natives do*." If some of those who think so, would only remember that this was the very way in which *they* learnt English, and then examine, in sober earnest, how much they really know about it, the delusion would vanish : they would find that the tables are turned, and that, on the contrary, if they would understand their own language *well*, they must consent to lay aside the " *native*," and commence learning *that, de novo*, in the very way foreigners do.* It is, in fact, desirable to strip our-

* Suppose you are asked, What is the French for "How do you do ?"—of course you say, "Comment vous portez-vous ?"—but if you are further asked, "What *is* Comment vous portez-vous, in English ?" and you still answer, "How do you do ?" you are badly taught; you have learnt French " *as the natives learn it ;*" i.e. ἀβασανίστως, ἀταλαιπώρως and (malgré fluency and Parisian accent) *perniciously* with regard to the *main* point, the PHILOSOPHY OF LANGUAGE. The youngest child who is taught this phrase, should *at the same moment*, be told that the French, instead of saying, "How do you do ?" say, "*How you carry you?*" i.e. "How do you carry yourself?" And so of all other idiomatic expressions. The opportunity of learning French conversationally, is, I allow, a great privilege : only let it be used aright, as an aid to the thoughtful study of the language, and not rested in, as if it were all in all. How many "Natives" there are, who, though well-informed and eloquent on other topics, are quite at a loss to explain the structure of their own simplest phrases. Now this is not the kind of knowledge I want, *educationally*, though of great value for other purposes.

Much more might be said on the study of modern languages, which I purpose, D.V., to follow up in a future Number (of *Classical Museum*.)

selves of our old slovenly habit of familiarity with mother-tongue, as a downright hindrance to accurate and scientific acquaintance; and, in the shirt-sleeves of conscious ignorance, to set about the M'Adamizing task of ascertaining what it is—*soit la prose, soit le vers*—that we have been all this time chattering and scribbling so complacently. Many, however, are never undeceived as to the actual amount of their knowledge; and, satisfied with an off-hand, negociable *connaissance* of their own language, they naturally, in the acquisition of a new one, make a similar acquaintance the *ne plus ultra* of their desires.   It is even a matter of regret and surprise to them, that Greek and Latin cannot be " picked up " on the same easy terms.   And, in fact, there have been ingenious attempts, such as " Corderius his Colloquies," to engraft classic lore upon our youngsters in this chit-chat, made-easy fashion.   All such attempts, besides ending in failure, betray, *in limine*, a misapprehension of *one* main purpose for which, as a matter of education, languages ought to be learnt at all.   If this were *merely*, as Rivarol seemed to think, in order to have " three or four different ways of expressing the same thing," (a power, by the bye, not at all to be despised), then, undoubtedly, the quickest, easiest, and cheapest way of getting up a vocabulary and phrases is the best; and the plodding scholar, " qui multa tulit fecitque puer, sudavit et alsit," is to be pitied for a sad waste of time, labour, and expense.   On the contrary, I have long been persuaded that, though many and great are the *direct* advantages resulting from the study of classics, yet these are all surpassed by the *indirect:* the incomparable training of the mind; the constant yet varied gymnastic exercise of memory, judgment, comparison, taste, order, investigation, &c.; the curious insight into the machinery of the human mind, and the operations of thought; and the interesting light thrown by the very idioms upon the character, customs, political and physical circumstances of nations ;—all included *in the mere process* of learning the languages. So that, if it were possible to deprive a *well-trained* scholar of every word of his Greek and Latin, and yet leave unimpaired the *mental power* acquired during the course of these studies alone, he would still be a *great* gainer by his classical education ; and might tell you that, though robbed of two precious jewels, he had still *by far the best half* of the treasure in his possession. I am well aware that this view of the *indirect* benefits of classical instruction is not the popular one ; nor would it, in fact, be at all true, if applied to the *kind* of classical instruction too often given, which may well justify *cui-bono* queries as to its possessing *any* value, direct or indirect. If, however, utilitarians would consider how many really great and wise men were produced in past ages, when the dead languages were cultivated to an *extreme* and *exclusive* extent, they must surely allow some *extraordinary* virtue, some " mighty magic," to a branch of learning which could, almost single-handed, achieve so much for the human intellect. How much more then, if only employed, as strenuously, in due proportion with other subjects! Yet it is to be feared that a sound, critical knowledge of the languages is increasingly undervalued in England, from an undue, short-sighted eagerness for those departments of knowledge which more immediately and *obviously* bear upon "the business of life;" as if any amount of what is called " practical knowledge " could supersede the necessity for training the reasoning powers to a *right application* of this mass of facts! Nay, to turn from the million, are we *quite* sure that, even at head-quarters, lax construing, " cram," " sciencing," &c., have not already (1850) begun to

replace the sterner requirements of philological accuracy ?*
I have seen books, and heard of lectures, that betoken
something *very* like it.   In this state of things, I venture
to offer a few remarks on the study of language, tending,
(I hope,) to promote that "*sound* learning" to which the
two Universities so emphatically pledge themselves.   These
remarks I especially commend, as "an elder soldier," to
those who are *commencing* a post-mortem examination† of

* Lest I should be misunderstood, I here beg to express my deep
regret for having in my younger days neglected, under the contemptuous
name of "cram," *much valuable information;* and to warn my young
readers of the sad and irreparable consequences of wilfully omitting *any
part whatever* of the duty before them *now*—the time appointed for
these things.   It is a part of God's providence that youth is, ordinarily,
the *only* time when some branches of learning are attainable; and it is
quite possible, through *culpable* neglect, so to mar one's education that
high attainment in some things shall only render the sense of ignorance
in others the more trying, because more keenly appreciated.   The
maxim, "these ought ye to have done, and *not to leave the other undone,*"
is, like many portions of the blessed word of God, capable of a *very*
general application.

My dear young Friends, listen to an *Old Bird*.   Leave Optimism
to the good citizens of Utopia and Laputa—take things as you find
them prepared to your hand—rough and smooth, bitter and sweet,
together.   ["The mixture, *as before*"—we ancients have all had to take
it, nolentes volentes.]   And though bad is the best in many human
arrangements, yet, for want of better, *make the best of it*.   It may be
good enough, "with care," for you at present, till times and systems
mend.   Meanwhile, be assured that almost *any* system, industriously
and cheerfully worked, will surpass the very best, taken up daintily and
fastidiously; and, if you find any *appointed* studies distasteful at first,
be sure to bestow *extra* application there, to overcome this feeling *as a
fault in yourselves*.   These are homely remedies for mental dyspepsia,
and may save repentance in after life.   Experto credite.

† My worthy Printer has, by calling my attention to a *faux pas*
here, enabled me to caution learners against an error in composition,
condemned in that excellent work, *Jani Ars Poetica*, p. 399.   In point

the languages of Greece and Rome. I will not stop here to prove the importance of WRITTEN TRANSLATION to the formation of a critical scholar. Every one knows the value of the practice: those who have most profited by it, best know the difficulties of the execution, *i. e.* " scribendi *recte*, nam ut *multum*, nil moror."

If one hundredth part of the time and trouble that has been mis-spent in preparing ready-made translations " in usum studiosæ juventutis" had been devoted, as by Mr. T. K. Arnold, to the task of putting them in the way of translating effectively *for themselves*, how much less should we have to deplore at the present day! The only *use* I can conceive for even a first-rate English translation at school, is for the pupils to hear it—with a feeling of curiosity and sympathy, not of indigence—read aloud by the Teacher, after the original passage has been well studied, and actually mastered. The *abuse* of it, and the employment in any way of second and third rates, can do nothing but harm. If the translation be a " free" one, it ministers to the natural eagerness to catch the general meaning without the trouble—the profitable toil—of honestly fighting one's way to it through the author's words. If *really* " literal," what nonsense it must be, every now and then! But—who *ever* saw a literal translation in print? Even Mr. Hamilton's are often far from it, in order to make sense.

of fact, "jucundissime Martialis," a *soldier* never *does* make a "post-mortem examination;"—small leisure for that, methinks, in the field! But, as "elder *surgeon*" would murder my quotation, and as I am partial, for the sake of old Bone Clarke reminiscences, to the "junctura" of post-mortem with *dead* languages, (Greek and Latin being in every sense "stiff ones"), I beg indulgence for the mixture of metaphors. Dr. Butler used to laugh at Horace for a similar fault, in playing at once the part of Bull and Bulldog, in *Epode* VI.

In making one's own translations for philological improvement, or for examination, I conceive the grand desiderata are—First, So to comprehend the *sense* and *force* of the author's ideas, as to transfer them, without loss of either, into any other language, as English. Second, So to appreciate the *form* into which *his* idiom has compelled him to throw those ideas, as to give the nearest possible approach to *this* in English also. Neither of these *alone* will convince an examiner that the student knows, "Marte suo," *exactly* what he is about: and the difficulty is, to combine the two, distinctly and intelligibly. For this purpose, I recommend an *interlined* version, in which the current, unbroken text shall convey the *force* of the original; whilst, *here and there*, a spare line above shall exhibit (as nearly as English can approximate, whether it "makes sense" or not,) the author's *way* of saying the same thing in *his* language, wherever the latter, *precisely* translated, deviates from the plain meaning in English. The learner should, in general, study to avoid the necessity for this upper line, by contenting himself with a sound, homely English rendering in the *current text*, and not making the two languages part company merely for the sake of *elegance* (this can, and must, be studied elsewhere), only most jealously recognising the minutest shade of *idiomatic* difference. In order to execute this plan, some precise system of notation should be rigidly adhered to. I therefore annex the following HINTS, which have been printed separately, for convenience.

HINTS

FOR "COMPARATIVE TRANSLATION,"

AS AN AUXILIARY TO ANY OTHER PLAN OF STUDY.

A METHOD equally applicable to all Languages; recommended, 1st, as an occasional exercise for Students of either sex: [not on any *a priori* theory; but as having grown up, bit by bit, out of the *necessities* of Students closely pressed for Philological accuracy;] 2ndly, in due proportion, for School, College, and other Examinations, where it defeats "crammed" Candidates; 3rdly, to Commentators, as the most concise means of elucidating difficult idiomatic passages; 4thly, *to practical Linguists, for working Philological and Ethnological problems.*

Dr. LATHAM has kindly permitted the following extract from private letters:—

"Some time back, my own attention was directed to the difficulty of obtaining a translation which should *at once* be verbally and grammatically accurate, and, at the same time, idiomatic. This was with reference to the examination papers at Cambridge. * * * Like yourself, I came to the conclusion that they were *incompatible*: for *two* purposes you must have *two* renderings. I quite agree with the general principles involved in your method."

Since then, he has given still more decided proofs of approbation.

The late Rev. T. K. ARNOLD also *strongly* commended, by letter, the employment of "Comparative Translation" to classical teachers, as follows:—

"I think the plan likely to be very useful, if adopted *entirely at first*, and occasionally afterwards." He subsequently inserted a favourable notice of it in his *Theological Critic.*

But the highest praise was that of Archbishop Trench.

DIRECTIONS FOR COMPARATIVE TRANSLATION.

First, having noted Page, Chapter, &c., on ruled paper, with ample margin, make a *plain* English version [*punctuation accurate*], without sacrifice of the author's sense or force, leaving the alternate lines blank. Next, above this version [and just *below* these spare lines], exhibit, *in blue ink or blue pencil*, and in as literal English *as possible*, irrespective of "making sense," every tangible difference of Idiom in the two languages; with remarks, where needed, in the margin; as follows:—

" Au lieu d' entrer dans des discussions critiques sur le merite des auteurs modernes, qui m' ont precédé dans ce genre d' ecrire, je me contenterai de faire quelques remarques sur les principales beautés de l'Apologue."—*Preface to Perrin's Fables.*

COMPARATIVE TRANSLATION OF THE ABOVE:

Instead of entering in(to) critical discussions on the merit of-the modern authors who have preceded me in this kind of writing, I shall be satisfied with making some remarks on the principal beauties of the Apologue.

The above translation illustrates *at once* the five principal rules given below; to which any additions may be made by convention between Teacher and Pupil, for their own convenience.

RULE I. Underline the words corresponding to each blue ink interlineation; to define, by way of "vinculum," or "brace," the precise *extent* of such correspondence. N.B.—Emphatic words may be *doubly* underlined.

Example. Au lieu = In stead. Tu ab urbe condita incipis. = Thou beginnest from the foundation of Rome.

RULE II. Whenever you have to express a single word in the original, by two or more words in the translation, connect the latter with *horizontal* hyphens, when close together, as, Erit = will-be; or with *converging* hyphens, when they are parted by other words, as, Non erit = will, not ,be.

Ex. Des = of-the. Lapides colligendi, quos Caius non videt.

= Stones to-be-collected, which Caius does, not ,see.

RULE III. Enclose between *curved* brackets ( ) all words not expressed in the original; reserving vertical braces [ ] for actual parentheses.

Ex. Dans = in(to). Homo [ut fama est] ab urbe venit.
= (A) man [as (the) report is,] came
from (the) city.

RULE IV. Suspend in a curved line, or *loop*, whatever is in the original, but is dispensed with in the translation.

Ex. Dans des discussions critiques. = Into *of the* critical discussions.

Ante quam Caius rediit. = Before *than* Caius returned.

RULE V. Two [or three ?] words, whose order is *essentially* different, may, occasionally, have small numerals *below* them, *besides* a *short* underline.

Ex. Discussions critiques = Critical discussions.
2   1

Τοῦτο δὲ δοκεῖ. = But this seems.
2   1

Also, in aid of the numerals, *u* (for *ultima*), and *p* (for *penult*), serve to mark, when needful, the *two last* words in a clause, as Cæsar exercitum parare cæpit = Cæsar began to-prepare an army.
u   p

Again, *i* (for *initial*) denotes the *first word*, as Priùs venit Cæsar quam expectavissent = Cæsar came sooner than they had expected.
i

And, "critical discussions" is shorter than "critical discussions";
r   2   1
the *r* meaning *reversed*.

N.B.—To ensure separate attention to the "two purposes" without distraction, the current text should be written first, without interruption, in convenient portions; the duplicate renderings, with *all* extra symbols, being reserved as after-work; and every word and mark superadded to the first version should be made conspicuous by *blue ink* (or else blue pencil), the practical advantage of which is considerable. *Red* is the established medium of *correction.*—See p. 22.

MISCELLANEOUS SAMPLES, SHOWING THE APPLICABILITY OF THIS METHOD TO TRANSLATION AND *RE-TRANSLATION*, FROM *ANY* EXERCISE BOOKS, IN *ANY* LANGUAGE.

Ex. 6.   Il comptait son argent tous les jours. = He
<u>was-counting</u>   <u>all the days.</u>
used to count his money every day.

Conversely.—He used to count his money every day. =
<u>usait à compter</u>   <u>tout jour.</u>
Il comptait son argent tous les jours.

Ex. 7. {
I am speaking of myself. = Je parle de moi-même.
                                     suis parlant   *mon-*

            Je parle de moi même. = I am speaking of myself.
                                    speak   *me-*

Ex. 8. {
Many dreadful things happen. = Πολλὰ (καὶ)
           πραγματα   *-ονται*

           δεινὰ   γὶγνεται.

           Πολλὰ καὶ δεινὰ γὶγνεται. = Many *and* dreadful
                     happens.
           (things) happen.

Ex. 9. {
What I have written must perish. = Quod
          ego habeo scriptum   *"must" perire.*
          scripsi   pereat necesse est.

          Quod scripsi pereat necesse est. = What
                   may-perish needful is.
          (I-)have-written must perish.

Ex. 10. {
Ich bin krank gewesen. = I *am* have been sick.
                                  2   1

            I have been sick. = Ich bin krank gewesen.
                           habe
                                       r

COROLLARY.—Observe how, in *re*-translation, as a natural consequence, the black and blue inks change places; and so do the numerals: the hyphens vanish, (though new ones may appear,) the bracketed words become looped, and *vice versa*. These changes, however obvious in theory, should be *realized by repeated practice*.

OBSERVE.—In the translations of examples 1, 6, 7, 8, 9, 10, we see by the *lower* line what the author *meant;* and by the *upper* how he *said* it. The latter has been called the "*Structural Translation*" by Dr. LATHAM.—It should be such a *picture* of the original as *never to mislead a stranger* as to the form or idiom of an *unknown* language.

For further illustration see Appendix, p. 41, or *Classical Museum* (Taylor and Walton, London) three articles "On the study of Languages," in Nos. 24, 25, 26; since reprinted, at the request of Dr. KENNEDY, as a separate pamphlet (same publishers, 1850).

ADDITIONAL HINTS TO PUPILS,

ON THE ADVANCED METHOD OF WORKING COMPARATIVE TRANSLATION, ETC.

WHATEVER language you are learning, ancient or modern, make a translation into your native tongue daily, occupying a whole sheet of paper; but of any size, from note to foolscap. Let the two first pages be done quite *freely;* the two last *strictly.* Then treat pages 1 and 3 with "blue ink," by the FIVE RULES; [and page 4 also, only *omitting interlineation.*]

By this process, four different kinds of exercise will be produced; each for a special purpose. Page 1, to exhibit the widest diversity, and page 3, the closest approximation, of the two languages. Page 2, to serve for the unfettered practice of English style. As for page 4, it will best teach you to *feel,* by contrast, the inadequacy of a *single* line for securing *all* the requirements of Philology.

If you learn French and German, with Greek and Latin, translate and re-translate the same passage from one of the four languages interchangeably with the other three, as an occasional exercise, according to the FIVE RULES.

Also, practise "construing" [see p. 35, or Classical Museum, No. 26, page 482, or pamphlet, page 22,] from each of the four into the other three, strictly observing the idiomatic *order* and *grouping* of each. This especially assists what is popularly called "*thinking* in a given language."

3

The French sentence, " J' ai vu beaucoup d' or," must be *ordered* and *grouped* variously, for construing into the four following languages :—

1, for English.   J' ai vu—I have seen, beaucoup d' or— much gold.

2, for German.   J' ai — Jch habe, beaucoup d' or — viel golb, vu — gesehen.

3, for Latin.   Beaucoup — Multum, d' or — auri, j' ai vu —vidi.

4, for Greek.   Beaucoup d' or — πολυν χρυσον, j' ai vu — ἑωρακα.

N.B.—The *reasons* of these several changes form a good lesson for young Philologers.

Whichever of these four languages you do *not* learn, at any rate inform yourself, from a good grammar, of some of the leading subjects of comparison in it ; under such heads as Article—Auxiliaries—Cases—Moods—Tenses—Aorist— Reflectives—Middle Voice—Separable Particles—Negatives —Numerals : which last are best appreciated by saying the multiplication Table in the strange language frequently, and with increasing rapidity, *i.e.,* " against time."

Any other language will serve ;—Welsh eminently: but I mention French and German as standard auxiliaries to a liberal and sound education.

I need hardly add that an earnest classical student must have a large amount of daily employment *besides* " Comparative Translation."   Such as, Greek and Latin verses (sense or nonsense), in the standard metres.   Turning verse into prose, and *vice versa.*   Ancient Geography and History, &c.   Filling up parsing tables, in columns.   Making notes and collecting examples, under heads *already entered* in an alphabetic Common-place book.   Learning by heart *select* portions of classical and English poets *and prose-writers.*

Arnold's and other exercises. Construing *aloud* passages from authors progressively more difficult. Collating, and marking with *mutual marginal references*, any two standard grammars, as Eton and Zumpt. Revising and macadamizing easy bygone school books, down to "Henry's First" and Delectus. Comparing a single verse of the Greek and Latin Testament daily with several cognate languages, as German, Dutch, Flemish, Swedish, Danish, Norse, Icelandic, and Faroese; or French, Italian, Spanish, Catalan, Portuguese, Enghadine, and Provençal; or, again, Welsh, Gaelic, Erse, Manx, Breton, *Cornish* (?) and so on. (See p. 29, and Pamphlet, p.16.) These, and perhaps many other kinds, of linguistic work, each in its turn, will profitably and happily *employ* much of the time too often *killed*, under the name of " light reading." Duty, steadily pursued, soon becomes a pleasure : but, at any rate, "*killing* TIME" is a bad preparation for ETERNITY.

The Author will, with the greatest pleasure, revise, for any experimenter, a short translation done by the above five rules from any of the current languages; forwarded, (anonymously if preferred,) to 38, Watergate Street, Chester.

In the foregoing "HINTS FOR COMPARATIVE TRANSLATION" I purposely select *hackneyed* and simple instances : as for the notation, any tutor and pupil may invent a better for their own use. To novelty the method can have no claim *now*, (1850) since I have myself been teaching and recommending it, in all essentials, for some years. But, wherever it is adopted *systematically*, and carried out, *in all its bearings*, with increasing precision, I will venture to answer for its *utility*.

I speak thus confidently, from corroborated experience; for this method does but embody, tangibly and attainably, a part of the characteristic spirit of SHREWSBURY TRAINING, which for so long a period *carried all before it* at both Universities: [" Ουδε πω ληξαντ' έχει:" witness the University Calendars, and the Catalogue prefixed to a fragrant *Salopian Bouquet*, entitled "SABRINÆ COROLLA." Geo. Bell, London, 1850.] My own obligations to that invaluable training I never could overstate: and I am sure my *old** Pupils will recognise, in "Comparative Translation," the pith of those principles, now systematized, which I used in those days " bonis lateribus suadere;" and with *some* success, though embarassed by a notation insufficient for the "two purposes." (*See* page 13.) I would now as soon lay aside Arabic figures, and teach long division with Roman numerals, as attempt to inculcate sound views of Philology without *black and blue* versions. See *Walker's Philosophy of Arithmetic*, page 2. lxvii.cccclxxxix÷dviii!!

Modern Languages may be translated on the very same plan with the greatest advantage; nay, I am convinced that such a mode of treatment imparts to them a con-

---

* I may be excused, on professional as well as friendly grounds, for adding here the names of Weldon, Whiston, Burrowes, Francis, [who have all since been Head Masters of Schools] Aspinall, M. Smith, Helps, Gathorne Hardy, T. Webster, Lukis, Denton, Robt. Williams, Golding, Proctor, Conybeare, Lawrence, James and Alexander Hildyard, Edgar Huxtable, Kempe, Ludlow, Paley, W. Martin, Lund, Overton, Groom, Allen, Harrison, Alex. Duncan, Metcalf, Myers, Jos. Noble, Constantine and Aug. Prichard, Wayte, Swayne, Joseph and Frederick Clarke, John Gray, Giles, Osler, Hamilton, Sykes, Dale, Scott, Gladstone, J. and K. Powles, Stevenson, Ll. Thomas, Semple, Watson, several Joneses, Daubenys, Foxes, and Johnstons; Johnson, Holden, Hodgson, Cearns, Dalton, Drysdale, Ayckbowm, Alexander, Wilson, Anderson, Kirby, Geo. Budd, D. Ker, Potts, McPherson, Carmichael, Radford, Willan, Tomlinson, Deane, Waterhouse, Haywood, Moore. Several more would oblige me by helping a *very* treacherous memory.

siderable portion of the "disciplinal value" of Greek and
Latin ; and would, if adopted earnestly in female education,
produce a very marked effect.   Nor can it be commenced
too soon, in principle ; although the written exercises must
be delayed till some manual dexterity is acquired.

Even very young children are amused to hear the droll
expressions which Frenchmen use, instead of speaking plain
English like other folks.   For instance, it seems somewhat
premature to say "I *have* cold," [J'ai froid,] before you
have *caught* it.   John Bull first catches his cold, and *then*
has it, like an honest man.

By and by, the "blue-inking" of Perrin's Fables becomes by no means so dry an operation as might be
supposed ; and the little folks are surprised into common-
sense Philology, before they are hardened into an inob-
servant use of their own mother-tongue.   This last, in turn,
becomes an object of interest and enquiry ; and, having by
this time "thought in French" a little, they begin to
observe what a funny language *English* is ; and how oddly
John Bull expresses himself now and then, *when one comes
to think of it.*   Thus it has been pleasantly argued, that the
best answer to "How do you *find* yourself?" would be,
"By hunting all about the room;" and to "How do you
do?" "I do as well as I can."

N.B—To ensure separate attention to the "two purposes" without distraction, the current text should always be
written first, without any interruption, in convenient portions ; the duplicate renderings, with the extra symbols,
being reserved as a separate task.   The *blue ink* is a *great*
improvement, suggested by a merry pupil (now "Matrona
potens"!)   It assists the eye and the mind, by exhibiting the
peculiarities of the original, not only in *alto relievo*, but in
glaring separation from that current text, wherein the two
languages have done their best to jog on *socialiter*, on a com-

mon line. [If the translation be submitted for *correction, this*
should be done, after the example of the late Dr. Tate of Rich-
mond, in *red* ink, which might also, pro re natâ, be used in the
first instance instead of the blue.]   In this way the " comparative anatomy," as it were, of the two languages, extinct
and recent, becomes an *unavoidable* study ; for the precise
limits of agreement and discrepancy must be carefully
sought before we put pen to paper.   Little idiomatic traits,
which are apt to escape the most watchful observer, are
actually *forced* upon the attention, and then impressed
upon the memory, by writing them down; and that in
a form peculiarly convenient for revisal, reference, or
retranslation, which should be introduced at proper intervals of time.   I believe no scholar, however matured,
could commence this mode of study without soon finding his
critical acumen sharpened, and discovering some phenomena
which had previously, in passing through a coarser sieve,
escaped his notice.

At the same time the principle is so perfectly simple,
and so natural a reply to a child's question about a new
language,—" What is the Latin for *the ?*" " What is the
French for *shall ?*" &c., that I do not hesitate to recommend
it, after trial, even in *the very earliest exercises.*   For
examples, see *Appendix*

To keep telling children, or teaching them rules, either
about the simple absence of the articles in Latin, or their
complicated use and omission in French and Greek, is one
of the most hopeless tasks ever undertaken ; whereas the
practical recognition of the same facts, in writing the
" structural translation," soon renders the said children perfectly familiar with the main principles ; leaving the rest to
be picked up with far less difficulty, (" leviora *tolli,*") as exceptions, often throwing light upon a rule which *they* already

understand, because, (with *proper* assistance,) they arrived at it for themselves, step by step, from facts and reasons.

On this and every account it is most desirable that, for the various languages, "first books" should be prepared, *exactly* corresponding, lesson by lesson, with each other, in all points where the languages themselves coincide; having separate extra chapters only when absolutely needful, viz., to illustrate the features peculiar to each. The very use of such books in *any* way, under circumstances ever so disadvantageous, would, of itself, work a great Philological reform. At present, the wanton dissimilarity, in plan and terms, between the Grammars or Exercise books of any two languages, hinders the natural classification of facts, and actually produces a false impression, most inimical to the cause of true scientific scholarship.

I have used, above, the popular expression, "thinking in French;" but I doubt much whether it is philosophically accurate. It seems to me that, whenever our thoughts run into language at all, we are doing something more than merely thinking; viz., translating our thoughts rapidly into English, French, &c.; in fact tacitly *talking* to ourselves in those languages.

The intimate and inveterate connexion of words with our thoughts, perhaps renders it, from long habit, very difficult for us to practise thinking without their aid,* or to detect ourselves when we *are* doing so; but I should be thankful for any hint from friends who may think it worth their while to observe such phenomena.

But it is in unstudied, involuntary mental operations that results are most to be depended on; and this is a subject on which one is *particularly liable to self deception.*

By "thinking in French," "thinking in German," &c., *to any purpose,* I understand *consciously* throwing one's

* See Whately's Logic.

thoughts into a French or German shape,—projecting one's plane English ideas upon the hill and dale of a French or German surface ;—standing, as it were, in a Frenchman's or German's shoes with regard to the expression of such and such a notion. To be able to do so, even to a very limited extent, is a *great* help towards acquiring their respective languages ; and I quite agree with those who, by the aid of foreign books, teachers, and conversation, endeavour to engraft *this* mental habit upon their children. A further, and higher exercise of the same habit is to take a Frenchman's or German's view of a Greek or Latin sentence ; to realize his conception, and sympathize with his *feeling*, of its peculiarities and difficulties.

To do this last with facility, on all occasions, would imply a *real* knowledge of the four languages, such as every professed scholar should be taught, in these days,* to aim at.

* In my time, those who knew a little German, even at College, were considered rather as phenomena ; besides being fair game for an occasional soi disant " Baron." And I am astonished that England has not, even yet, seen the expediency of making French and German a matter of course in Leading Classical Schools ; instead of leaving them to the few volunteers who furnish no adequate remuneration for *competent* Foreign Teachers. The *direct* benefit of such studies is now (1850) increasingly great, from the extension of British intercourse with foreign countries. But, independent of this, would not general scholarship receive a great impulse, from the study of additional analogies ? Not, certainly, if each of the five grammars were learnt *as a separate science*. But the Principals could first enforce, with *educated* Professors, the rational amount of uniformity for all ; and then consolidate the whole, by express instruction in Universal Grammar.

If such training as this became general, I believe it not only *might* bring out, here and there, a latent Grimm or Bopp, now lost to Science —for true Philology *is* a science—but *would* certainly raise the temperature of our average Scholarship by many degrees. I commend the suggestion *strongly* to the attention of those who have the power to act upon it.

But the mere habit of using, from imitation, a certain set of French or German phrases, as naturally as English, without the process of translation from the latter, though highly valuable as a means to an end—as data to work upon,—rather deserves the name of *chatting*, than of *thinking* in those languages, unless some intelligent analysis and comparison be superadded.

As the *Classical Museum* is no doubt much read by classical *Teachers*, some of them may take alarm at a plan which seems to militate against their profession, by proclaiming, "GREEK AND LATIN WITHOUT A MASTER." Now, in the first place, ὅπερ σαφεστάτη πίστις, *I am myself in the trade.* Secondly, I can assure them, that though *any* one can pursue this method of translation "after a fashion," and with *some* benefit, yet to do it *well* is the most difficult task I have ever yet attempted; a task beset with sifting niceties, stimulating to the tyro, humiliating to the veteran; above all, *eminently requiring correction!* Τεκμήριον δέ. I have now before me two large packets of such translations arrived by post, *blue inked* by my pupils, and to be returned *red inked* by me, with marginal annotations. Courage! mes camarades; *good* machinery gives employment to *more* hands eventually, in our workshops, as in others.

I have endeavoured to impress upon my readers, ἄλλους τε καὶ τοὺς νεωτέρους, that, in studying a language, the grand object should be, not so much learning to talk, write, or read, as learning to *think:* and I suggested a plan for translating, which should render a little thinking *absolutely inevitable*, and thus help to cure that pernicious habit of vague rendering which is too often, not merely permitted, but even encouraged, and that too in places "pollicitis meliora." The essentials of this plan are, that the author's

4

meaning should first be secured in *plain* English; and that, wherever the said plain English deviates from the author's *idiom*, there, *and there only*, the closest possible English imitation of that idiom (whether in phrase, mood, tense, or *anything else whatever*), should be also given above the line, and in blue ink; taking care to underline, by way of vinculum, the corresponding part in the lower line. See *Appendix*, for samples of such translation; I cannot say done to my mind, for *that* is, "qualem nequeo monstrare, et sentio tantum;" but perhaps calculated to illustrate the method more effectually than the scraps given in the *Hints.* With regard to the merits of the system, some one may say, "Est istuc quidem aliquid, sed nequaquam in isto sunt omnia." To this I so entirely assent, that, though the method is a pet of mine, yet I would not have it supersede *any one* of the various kinds of exercise already in use. All I would contend for is, that neither should any of *them* supersede *it;* and, for pupils who have much inaccuracy to unlearn, it ought for a time to form the "staple." It is not a few dips of blue ink that will suffice to counteract *years* of slovenly rendering; and I have seen lads and lasses for whom, on our first interview, I should order a quart bottle at once.

There is a real difficulty in the application of such a minute system as "Comparative Translation" to large classes in Public Schools, namely—the impossibility of correcting a great number of such exercises with sufficient accuracy. This, however, is but a part of the general difficulty which, with many advantages, attends that kind of education; where, in most branches of tuition, an approximation to individual attention is all that can, with the best management, be attained. Therefore, as many other great difficulties are, by educational tact and industry, got over at Public Schools, the only question with me is, *how* to get over *this* difficulty; for, if "Comparative Translation" have but one-fifth of the virtue I ascribe to it, it *must* be got over, by hook or by crook.   Now, in the first place—I would rather have ever so short an exercise, even copied down from dictation, than omit the practice altogether. Secondly—A few lines only of each translation might be "blue inked," leaving the rest *au naturel.* (See the AD-DITIONAL HINTS TO PUPILS.)   Thirdly—Some of the best translators in the class might, after having their own exercise corrected, be at once doing and getting good, by revising the rest, and "obelizing" faults to guide the master in deducting marks.   Fourthly—A class might be subdivided, so that each group of four or five should concoct one exercise amongst them, liable to the check of individual questioning.

I am sure I have not exhausted the methods by which a teacher, as thoroughly convinced as I am of the benefit of these exercises, might contrive to introduce them, even for the largest classes.   But, after all, it must be confessed that Comparative Translation can only be fully carried out in *private* tuition; and here the above "concocting" method might answer well for a junto of fellow-students, who, after doing their utmost to criticise each other, might send the result of their convergent acumina to a private tutor for the *coup de maitre.*   Lector benevole, ridebis, et licet rideas; for this outbreak of the "puff indirect," I plead the JUS TRIUM LIBERORUM, which I have long learned to translate "Kail* for three bairns."

The pupils, when once initiated, should by all means practise occasional versions from Greek and Latin into French, German, &c., on the same principle, with retranslations from these again, as well as from English.   By such

* Est operæ pretium *duplicis* cognoscere juris Naturam.—HOR,

means, modern languages may become valuable auxiliaries, instead of being a trivial interruption to the graver studies, as is too often the case, *solely* from an irrational method of studying them. (*For Examples, see Appendix.*)

There is another very simple plan by which the philosophy of language may be made interesting to the young. Suppose a family, or class, who have all begun French, and one of whom knows a little Greek and Latin : lay open on a desk a row of Testaments, in the cognate languages, Latin, French, Italian, Spanish, Portuguese. Let the " Scholar" translate aloud, verbatim, and *in its own order*, a single verse of the Greek Testament, bit by bit, whilst the juniors, in turn, check this rough translation by reading each bit after him, from the Authorised Version. This alone is enough to produce an interest, even in *very* young minds, about the difference in the Greek *idiom*, though dressed in English words; and the strangeness of the rhetorical order, compared with the simple metaphysical order of the English ; with judicious remarks and management, I believe it might even facilitate the *learning* of Greek by and bye. But more will be done, if the same verse be translated (or even puzzled out ever so lamely, by analogy) in the cognate languages in succession; the business of the juniors *then* being to listen for words which, perhaps with some modification, run through all or most of the open books. Let one such word be selected daily for entry in a sheet ruled into columns, as below. The whole occupies fifteen or twenty minutes. If there are German students in the class, open another row of German, Dutch, Swedish, Danish, and Icelandic Testaments, and use them, on alternate days, in the same way. Of course, the rows might, according to the pursuits of the class, consist of any other families of languages, as the Celtic, Slavonic, or Semitic,

Teutonic.	*English*	*German*	*Dutch*	*Swedish*	*Danish*	*Icelandic*
	Soul	Seele	Ziele	Sialan	Siel	Sal

Romish...	*English*	*French*	*Italian*	*Spanish*	*Portug'se*	*Latin*
	Jews	Juifs	Giudei	Judios	Judeos	Judæi

Celtic.....	*English*	*Welsh*	*Gaelic*	*Erse*	*Manx*	*Breton*
	Heaven	Nefoedd	Néamh	Neamh	Niau	Eon

The number of languages, however, would only *increase* the sphere of action. The thing is quite practicable in principle, and well worth attempting, where nothing is actually learnt but French, which presents with four other languages numerous plain analogies, such as the quick ear of children readily appreciates; and some, who have not yet begun even French, might listen to the rest with prospective benefit. It is a great thing to have the mind early opened to the consideration of LANGUAGE, *as such.* Nor is the general benefit by any means confined to etymology; an intelligent teacher may call attention to *any* of the phenomena of language, as they present themselves; and thus lay a foundation for more rational ideas of grammar afterwards, when it comes to be *learnt.* I am well aware that some will object to such a practice, as tending to confuse the mind, and prevent a distinct apprehension of *any* language. I believe such objectors are not aware of the extreme aptitude of the infant mind for language, when presented simply and judiciously, *i. e.*, in other words, *naturally.* Professor Newman informs me, that—" At Bagdad, Armenian boys often learn Turkish and Armenian from their childhood in their own families, and superadd Arabic from the community as they grow up. To know three languages (as Arabic, Turkish, and Persian) is not a *very* unusual accomplishment: Armenians sometimes know four. In Eastern Europe the phenomena are very similar; Hungarians know Magyar, German, and Slovak." Such results spring up, almost in

the school of nature, under favorable circumstances, such as
no educational system can imitate: but the facts may
remove a prejudice against presenting languages to children
at an early age ; and observe, in the case above suggested,
the great proportion of the languages are not supposed to
be *learnt* at all, but merely glanced at for the purpose of
philological comparison. The subject matter being happily
familiar—the individual phrases having been carefully dis-
sected out from the original—all difficulties removed—some
curiosity awakened—nothing exacted from the hearers but
attention, which is all but secured—I am convinced that
any number of *obviously cognate* languages [nay, even dialects and patois,* if time served] might be examined with
solid benefit to the *future* grammarians, though now in
the embryo or tadpole state.

Nor do I despair of even more important results still
from these little Scripture readings ; such minute attention
to the word of God in small portions may, if earnestly and
seriously carried on, be profitable, with His blessing, in the
best and highest sense, both to teacher and learners. Nor
can it fail to impress any candid mind with the sterling
value of the ENGLISH AUTHORISED VERSION, compared with
any other. Such readings, however, should not, on any
account, assume the rank of a *religious exercise ;* they may
conspire, but must not usurp. The vernacular is the language to reach the heart.

* The patois, or genuine provincial dialects of any language, (exclu-
ding artificial " slang "), are by no means to be despised: they very often
throw light on Philology, by supplying defective forms, and deciding
doubtful analogies. I used to identify the French *car* with γαρ, till my
friend Mr. Suliot told me he had seen it spelt *quar* (for *quare*), as it is
also in " *La Bible des Pauvres*," in the various readings. See Ampere sur
l'origine de la Langue Française ; Gilly's Romaunt Version of St. John's
Gospel, and various works in the Catalogue de la Linguistique of
Théophile Barrois, 13, Quai Voltaire, Paris.

I believe the rules and specimens given (see *Appendix*) will serve to explain in general my proposed method of "black and blue" *translation for philological purposes.* But, as any such illustration is necessarily inadequate, I should be very glad to receive from any working philologer (student or tutor), a *short* idiomatic passage of prose Greek, or Latin, &c., translated *with minute attention to the five rules,* and with ample margin. In this way the "*whys*" and the "*why-nots*" which may arise in thinking minds can be answered by correction and comment, more effectually than by any amount of printing, on a subject which, from its nature, *can* only be fully appreciated *in the working.* In reply to some questions already raised, I will just observe, 1*st*, that it is by no means intended to supersede oral instruction. On the contrary, the revisal of such a translation with the pupil, is apt to lead to *much* vivâ voce comment, and inculcation of principles. It is true, several of my pupils have thought it worth while to receive instruction by correspondence, marginal notes being then used as a substitute for the said "vivâ voce;" in which way, though less is done in a given time, yet what *is* done becomes more precise and fixed: "litera scripta manet," whereas oral remarks too often not only penetrate, but actually *traverse* the cranium, "demissa *per* aures," without leaving a trace of their passage! 2*ndly*, That this system admits of *no* deviations, *no* exception of any cases as "trifling," or "too well known to require repeated notice." Its novelty and supposed value consist in attempting, in addition to a *good* translation, to exhibit, visibly and intelligibly, *every* existing difference between the two languages. It requires the pupil, instead of omitting familiar facts, and only noticing fresh cases, to shew, in black and white, and *blue,* all the phenomena he can possibly detect; and, therefore, it ascribes, in fierce *red*

ink, the smallest omission either to ignorance or careless-
ness.   As the tyro advances, he ought, instead of relaxing,
to prove his advancement by greater attention to minutiæ ;
and the premium should always be on *increased* accuracy.
Let all sorts of other exercises be used, each for its own
effect ; but let me have *this* rigidly followed out, as the
proper instrument for inducing philological research—the
"*Natur-forschung*" of language—and I will venture to say,
the result will not disappoint *on the whole*, though I will
not stop to prove a separate *cui bono* for each instance
of hyphen or bracket.   It is the habit of *unremitting,
invariable* watchfulness that is valuable, as a means to an
end ;   that end being not to obtain "*toties quoties*," some
fresh information, nor merely to learn the respective idioms
of Greek, Latin, French, &c., but by a sifting observation,
of the facts of each *in turn* and *inter se*, to establish an
extensive and growing INDUCTION, through which the learner
shall arrive, by his or her own discoveries, at the laws—
logical, etymological, grammatical, metaphysical, &c.,—
which would constitute, when attained, the true philosophy of
language :—" Enfin, on nomme 'Grammaire comparée' la
science qui enseigne à comparer la structure de la phrase
dans une langue avec la structure de la phrase dans une
autre langue.   La grammaire comparée peut enseigner ainsi,
non seulment une langue inconnue au moyen d'une langue
connue, mais encore à comparer les formes de deux ou
plusieurs langues, et *à tirer de cette comparaison des in-
ductions utiles au progrès des connaisances humaines.*"
[*Grammaire Français Expliquée au moyen de la langue
Provençale.*   Marseille, 1826, page 2 ; in many respects a
very sensible book.]

The very object in view, therefore, excludes *any wilful*
omission.   A translation from Latin, *not* bracketing (" a ")

and (" the "), or *not* hyphening " I-have-loved," (=amavi)
would be *directly opposed* to the system above recommended.   Equally so, a translation from *French,* hyphening " I
have loved " (=j'ai aimé) or not " looping " the article in
"*the* virtue," (from *la* vertu).   In each case, there would be
a virtue denial of certain facts in the respective languages.
They may be called *small* facts ; but the presence or absence
of articles and auxiliaries are points of *some* interest, and
the student will one day be glad to have had them *forced*
upon his microscopic attention.   " Small facts " often mean
nothing less than those *important* facts which are *most apt
to escape notice;* and the old proverb, " take care of the
pence, and the pounds will take care of themselves," may be
applied here, mutatis mutandis, with great truth.   Without
introducing *wilful* omission, be sure that abundant difficulties will arise " in the working," to *compel* omissions, malgré
nous ; and here the *mind* is set to work, to overcome, to
escape, to approximate, &c.   Such " cruces " are the very
mines of our philological traffic, and they are happily of
frequent occurrence ; whilst the trifles and small facts serve
to " keep one's hand in," and one's eyes open, during the
intervals.   Once admit the omission of " simple cases," and
the language will grow in *simplicity* to a wonderful extent,
tyrone judice, till nothing will be deemed worthy of notice,
but such passages as have puzzled *him* or *her* to make out.
Now, these may be extremely barren in philological interest,
whilst a little question about attribute or predicate, which
to *them* presented no difficulty, [sure it "*made sense*" *either*
way !] may involve an important law of language.   No, my
young friends, our motto must be " no surrender," if we
are ever to make philologers of you at all ; consider *every*
point worth recognizing, if it be *a fact,* and you will soon
find that whilst all your difficulties become easier, some of

your facilities will become more difficult. What used, in the good old times, to go down once for all in the form of a *bolus,* will now be retained for repeated discussion and agitation,—" The *gargle* as before,"—each time as it occurs. It might be supposed that great sameness results from tying down all pupils to the same dry inexorable rules. On the contrary, it is most amusing to observe how each young mind cuts out, in spite of this* Logierian phrenoplast, *its own way* of doing the same *thing.* One will lean to *etymology,* and call ξύμμαχοι <u>allies</u>, abundare <u>to abound</u>, and so forth. Another is a great stickler for *order,* and must needs make his blue ink versions ultra-barbarous, by *placing* the words exactly as they stand in the original; he therefore renders γενήσεται δὲ ὑμῖν πειθομένοις καλὴ ἡ ξυντυχία—" But the coincidence will turn out favourable to you if you comply." One affects the metaphysical order, at a sacrifice of native force. Another struggles to retain the rhetorical order, till he becomes un-English. † No fear of *sameness,* where human *minds* are really *set to work* (which *is bonâ fide* the case in a " black and blue " translation,)—"mille adde catenas, "Effugiet tamen hæc sceleratus vincula Proteus :" [ne dicam, " Fiet aper."]

Ex re FABELLA.

THIS reminds me of the ingenious efforts I witnessed when a boy, on the part of two very refractory young point-ers, their object being to carry with them, ἑνί γε τῳ τρόπῳ,

* Logier invented the cheiroplast, a frame for keeping the fingers in the right posture, *per force,* in learning the piano-forte.

† These several tendencies should not on any account be checked at the outset, but rather *encouraged to the full,* and modified by degrees.

through the "sata læta boumque labores," a most for-
midable species of clog, contrived on purpose to keep them
from rambling. *Did* it, though? ὦ τύμπανα καὶ κύφωνες, οὐκ
ἀρήξετε; on the contrary, after a few self-taught lessons in
clog-driving, behold "Rumbo" and "Major" trundling
their impedimenta right merrily through *every* thing (not
excepting *standing beans*) αὐτοῖσι τύμπανοισι καὶ κύφωσι!
THE MORAL.—"What then, Patres conscripti? shall naugh-
ty little quadruped bow-wows * * * in a bad cause too
* * * ? and shall *not* good big biped Βου-παιδες in a
good cause * * * ?"—cæteraque gravissimè. [Cicero,
all over.]

ON PHILOLOGICAL CONSTRUING.

HAVING alluded to "loose construing" as *one* of the pests
of education, ("tum *variæ* illudent pestes,") I wish to enter
a little more particularly into the subject, as a *very* important one. Some are content with pupils giving the general
drift of the author, without any regard to the *words*
employed. To *make* them do this now and then, and do it
properly, is a very good practice; but to break off the
ready-made trick, the ordinary conjectural mode, would be
a boon to both tutor and pupil. I remember at school—I
mean *the* school—SHREWSBURY School—*be-grudging* the
trouble which Dr. Butler *always* inflicted on us, of separa-
ting the poor little enclitic "que," from its more powerful
friend. *We* would fain have said " Arma, arms, virumque,
and the man." But that very best of teachers would
insist upon " Arma, arms, *que and*, virum, the man."
It did not occur to "us lads," (though "hoc caverat
mens provida Reguli,") that, as we were turning *Latin*
into *English*, it behoved us, 1*st*—to bring the "and"

into its English and *logical* place; 2*d*, to shew up John Bull for *not having* a spare enclitic conjunction = "and;" 3*dly*, to mark the distinction between *this* "que" and the other *in*separable "que," of quisque, uterque, &c., a fruitful source of puerile blunders, as some of us remember to our *cost** I mention this, to illustrate the importance of picking and sorting individual words; the smaller and more insignificant the better, to establish a *principle*. As a general rule, *all* conjunctions should be taken alone. They are *links:* not, however, like the links of a chain, where all play the same part, but as distinct from that which they connect as pins are from the papers or ribbands which they fasten together; and they should be taken out, like pins, to *acknowledge* their distinctness. So should interjections, for the same *logical* reason. (See Latham's *First Outlines of Logic*, pp. 4, 21, 22, 30.) On the contrary, prepositions should not, without special reason, be detached from their nouns, with which they form the equivalent of a single word, —in fact, a " case" of the noun. " Caio" = " to-Caius" is, mentally, no more a single word then "ad Caium" = "to Caius." Adjectives, one or more, when performing the function of mere attributes or epithets, should accompany the noun; as "Roma ferox, fierce Rome," "ποδάρκης δῖος Ἀχιλλεύς, the swift god-like Achilles." But, when they appear in the more marked form of predicate, then they should be as carefully *separated* from their nouns. Fancy construing "candidum Soracte"—"the white Soracte!"—Hor. Od. 1, 9. Or "matrem armatam "—"the armed mother"— Virg. Æn. iv. 472.

The union or disunion of adverbs and verbs should also be regulated by similar considerations—by an appeal "ad

* Salopian Reader, didst ever get turned down with the lesson " in Greek and English?" If so, thou wilt duly appreciate the word " cost," h. l.

synesim," not by rule. "Ad benè vivendum," go very well
en masse. But in Hor. Sat. I. 4 13, I should take the trouble
of saying, "scribendi, of writing, rectè, properly;" because
scribendi is repeated from the preceding verse, and *then*
qualified by a *very* emphatic word "rectè," *worthy* of being
isolated. All vocatives, from their parenthetic nature,
should be eliminated, like interjections.

In this way, a "phrase," which has no true English
meaning but as an assemblage of various parts of speech,
becomes, by its escape from the customary dissection, *quite
a striking phenomenon:* a mind trained to impatience of
wholesale rendering, is thus led to examine *why* such and
such assemblages acquired their respective meanings; and
facts, great and "small," are rescued, which would escape
notice if grouping were the *rule*, instead of the exception.
To a slovenly construer, *every* parcel of words is equally a
"phrase," equally mysterious and inviolable; their separation, murder! Now I would have *accurate* construing,
(from *motives*, varying pro re natâ), made the constant
recognition, and therefore the constant practice and corro-
boration, of innate philosophical principles, à teneris unguibus. For I have learnt that *careless* construing operates,
most effectually, to the ignoring and confounding such
principles, till at last the mind becomes hardened against
their reception by the pernicious habit of "taking," (and
therefore *considering*) words in promiscuous bunches, as if
they had so much meaning *per dozen*, instead of acting
upon the fact, that "the parts of speech are determined by
the structure of propositions, and a word *is* a noun, a conjunction, or a verb, according to either the place it takes in
a proposition, or the relation it bears to one" (Latham, *ibid*,
p. 2.) By following up, in good scientific earnest, such a
process as "construing" *used* to be, one may hope to eluci-

date gradually the limits of the normal and the aberrant of language, and to deduce its pathology from its physiology, and *vice versa*.　　But I am often grieved by hearing even decent scholars *lumping* their words in a way that "we lads" should have smarted for, had we dared to take such liberties even in a " Greek and English" *imposition*.　　The natural consequence of such a practice must be, that many who pass for proficients in Greek and Latin (learnt *per se et propter se,*) are so little improved as rational beings, that practical thinking men, who fall in with such " young collegers," naturally question the utility of those dead languages.　　"*They* would never trouble their heads with such stuff."　　Nor, in fact, did the said " collegers."　　It was never an intellectual process at all with *them*.　　Their teachers inculcated; *they* devoured; and the result was—a *farrago*. (*Vide* all three words in an old Ainsworth : inculco, devoro, farrago.

ILLUSTRATIONS of the METHOD of COMPARATIVE TRANSLATION.

WITH regard to the Modern Languages, as I am not acquainted, even tolerably, with any but Welsh, French, and German, I beg indulgence for the sentences I have, with the help of Testaments and Dictionaries, adapted to the method, to demonstrate its universal applicability. I make no apology for introducing specimens of my native language, an auriferous vein of Celtic, which I only lament that I, in common with most of my countrymen, have worked sadly too little; whilst I condole with those English Linguists who, despising such a rich living mine close at hand, almost always " go farther and fare worse," in search of philological treasures.　　So do I condole with the Florist, who is too fond of Dahlias and Pelargoniums to have an eye for our own " Alaw wen " * and " Ffa corsydd." † And so perhaps some *literal* miners, who have exchanged Dolgelle for California, may now be singing "mae'r enaid yn Meirionydd," and wishing they had hammered on contentedly, "ym *mherfedd* gwlad Gwynedd gwyllt." The few non-native scholars who have studied Welsh at all— I may instance the present Bishops of Llandaff and St. David's, Rev. Joseph Baylee, Mr. Bruce Knight, Lady Guest, Professor Newman, and the late excellent Dr. Pritchard—have at least seen enough to be astonished at the general indifference of THE NATIVES to facts so truly interesting, καὶ ἤν ἐπιχώρια σφίσιν ῇ. Query, whether even the approaching RHUDDLAN EISTEDDFOD holds out any encouragement to critical research into the peculiarities of our mother-tongue ? (1850)

To have exhibited the different coloured inks would have been very difficult, with a great addition to the expense ; also, the *printing* of Comparative Translation in any way being extremely troublesome, and even when most successful, very *unlike the life,* I have on every account reserved the principal illustrations for an Appendix, in the form of autograph, by the aid of transfer paper. As to style, the exercises are just such as plodding Tyros might be expected to perpetrate for themselves, and the notation is, in its details, (some of which are proposed below), avowedly *provisional.* My first efforts at reform were still *more* clumsy ; I have kept " blundering on," gladly adopting the inventions of my pupils, and holding out (*now,* as much as ever) "Si quid novisti rectius." Some of the devices serve merely, ob differentiam, to distinguish one word, or form of word, from another, though the meaning be not sensibly affected ; not

* Water Lily, Nymphœa alba.   † Bogbean, Menyanthes trifoliata.

without a hope that the watchfulness thus induced may now
and then detect unsuspected shades of difference : *e. g.*
between the two Aorists. The delicacy and obscurity of
many other questions about tense and mood, render it
desirable to adapt the notation to that subject with especial
precision : and our present inability to represent adequately
some of these verbal relations shews the importance of
noticing and recording facts. The research and thought
brought to bear upon such " open questions " are amongst
the benefits which Comparative Translation is intended to
promote ; and the discussion of a point which seems, as to
the meaning of the particular sentence, the idlest in the
world, may be lending a little help to settle an important
general principle.

"Agamus igitur pingui Minerva ;" and, *for the present,*
let

$$\left.\begin{array}{l}\text{vocari} = \text{to-be-called.} \\ \text{vocandus} = \textit{having}\text{-to-be-called.}\end{array}\right\}\text{ob differentiam.}$$

This accords with one English use of the verb *Have*, in
both voices ; " I *have* to call " = vocandum est mihi ; and
" I *have* to be called " = vocandus sum.   Also, with the
Italian, Spanish, and Portuguese tenses—Ho da scrivere, I
have to write.   Havía de cantar, I *had* to sing.

Let τετυφως = having-stricken; τυψας = [1]having-
stricken ; τυπων = [2]having-striken ; τυπτομενος = being-
stricken ; τυφθεις = [1]stricken ; τυπεις = [2]stricken ; τετυμμενος
= having-been-stricken.

There are cases where the bracket and hyphen may be joint-
ly used : thus, let honores = (civic)-honors ; inimicus = a
(personal)-enemy ; because, whilst the adjective in each
forms no *essential* part of the noun's meaning, it is habit-
ually *implied*.   But homunculi = little-men, *without*
brackets ; Let Amas = (thou)-lovest ; since amas by

termination, denotes the 2nd person singular, yet does not actually *employ* tu = thou.   Let Tu amas = thou-lŏvest, to recognise both the emphasis, and what Dr. Latham calls "excess of expression." (*Outlines of Logic*, p. 32.)   Compare Moi, J'aime.   Toi, tu aimes, &c.

The "signs of cases" form a difficult and instructive subject for consideration.   Perhaps, Mr. Hamilton's method of selecting one typical preposition for each is the best : but of course, " looping" it up, whenever it is pleonastic, and *always* employing the hyphen.

If the above provisional postulates serve to set any young Philologers *a-thinking*, enough has been said to introduce

THE APPENDIX.

EXAMPLES OF COMPARATIVE TRANSLATION, APPLIED TO
" THE VERY EARLIEST EXERCISES."

N.B.—Some niceties are purposely omitted.

FRENCH.   La vertu = Virtue.   De la salade = Some salad.   Manger du fromage = To-eat cheese.   Un homme credule = A credulous man.   Pleasure = (Le) plaisir.   I am cold = J'ai froid.   A solid genus = Un genie solide. J'aurai = I shall-have.

* French, like other modern languages, supplies the want of a real Indefinite Article by the first numeral, "un, une."

6

LATIN. Balbus murum ædificat = B. is-building (a) wall.
₂ ₁

Puer vulpem non timet = (The) boy does. not ,fear (a) fox.

The boy was building a house = Puer domum ædificabat.
(the) (a) (erat ædificans)

I came to see you = Veni ut viderem te. Dixeram
(ego) (videre) (vos)
= (I)-had-said.

GREEK. *Βλάπτουσι σε* = (They)-are-injuring thee.

Φευγε τὴν ἀδικιαν = Avoid injustice. We are yielding to
(the)

force = *Εἴκομεν* (τῇ) *βιą.* Pursue both justice and virtue
(ἡμεις ἐσμεν ἐικοντες)

= *Δίωκε καɩ* (τὴν) *δὶκην κὰι* (την) *ἀρέτην.* He will hurt
(ἀμφω)

thee = *Βλαψει σε. Τυφθησόμενος* = about-to-be-beaten.
(* θελει βλαπτειν)

* In Modern Greek *θὲλω δώσει* = I will give = Ich werde geben.

GERMAN WITH FRENCH. (Ahn's exercises.) Ist der
Vater krank ? = Le pere est (il) malade ? Ich habe mein
(2) (1)

Buch verloren = J'ai perdu mon livre. Cet enfant est il
(2) (1)

ton frere ? = Ist dieses Kind dein bruder ? Beaucoup d'
(er)
(2) (1)

argent = viel geld.
(von)

In these examples, I have introduced some of the phenomena respecting the two articles, the auxiliaries, interrogatives, &c., which are
particularly striking to *children.*

LONGER SAMPLES OF COMPARATIVE TRANSLATION.

Cicero De Oratore I. 1.

Oftentimes when I [-in-number] am in deep [cogitating] thought and [to-me]

recollecting [reseeking in-memory] old (affairs), those (men), Brother Q., are wont

to-appear [to have been] very happy- [through-blessed] {= [highly favored]} who in (a) first rate [best] republic

(like ours), have-been-able, whilst flourishing [when they-might-flourish] both in- [and]

(civic)-honors, and in (the) renown of (their) exploits, [things carried-on]

to-maintain [hold] such [that] (a) course of-life, that they could live [might-be-able] [to-] either [or]

in business [an-leisure] without danger, or at leisure [in] with dignity.

And (there) was [† has been] (a) time when I used-to-think [was-deeming] (that)

to myself [to-me] also (a) beginning of-rest, and of-recalling [bearing-again] (my)

attention to my own [mind] and your [of-both] [of-us] noble [clear] pursuits, would be [to-be-about-to-be]

due [just] and conceded by almost [nigh] all, whenever [if] (the) endless [unended]

labor of-forensic affairs, and (the) occupation of-canvassing, [* going about]

{* or the-absorbing-pur-suits of ambition} might-cease, [-have-stood-together] from (the) completion [running-down] of

(my) (civic)-honors, as well [also] as (the) decline [from] [bend] of-life. [age]

† Latin has no Aorist *form.*

Thucydides I. 1.

Thucydides of ^{Athenian} Athens wrote-an-account-of ^{.with = together} the war

between ^{of,} the ‚Peloponnesians and Athenians, (describing)

^{as} how they-warred against each other; ^{to} ^{other-others} beginning (the nar- ^{having-begun}

rative) as soon as (it) was-set-on-foot, ^{straight} ^{being-set-down} and expecting (that it) ^{having-hoped}

would be both ^{to-be-about-to-be} ^{and} great, and more worthy of mention ^{most-word-worthy}

than all preceding ^{of-the} ^{before-having-become} (wars); conjecturing (thus) because both

(parties) were-at-their-height ^{= culminating?} for this war ^{* same} in-their whole ^{-the} ^{all}

equipment ^{preparation}; and seeing the rest of Greece siding with ^{other Grecian (?)} ^{being-set-t gether to} one-

or-other, some ^{the} indeed immediately, ^{straight} but others ^{the} also ^{and} inten-

ding (to do so). For this movement proved ^{became} (a) very serious ^{greatest}

(one) indeed to-the Greeks and to-some part of-the Bar-

barians, and one ^{but} may ^{as} say ^{to-say} also ^{and} to ^{on} (the) most (part)

of-mankind, for the ^{-men} (events) (immediately)-before them, and ^{* same}

those still ^{the} ^{yet} more-ancient were not ^{was} to be discovered, ^{imposs!bles} ^{to-have-found} clearly

at least, ^{indeed} through length ^{multitude} of-time.

* δ αυτος = *the* same.

* HELPS TO PARSING, &c.

The object of the Table (p. 46) is not to dispense with syntax rules, but to refer as many of them as possible to a few leading *principles.* The instances that will *not* fall in, [as DIGNUS, FUNGOR, &c.,] for that very reason claim *extra* attention and thought; especially in writing exercises.

The 3rd Concord may, by Cæsar's hint [Diem dicunt, quo *die,* &c.], be dispensed with in *parsing: not* in Exercises, where the pattern "Ego qui am*o,* Tu qui am*as,* Ille qui am*at,* &c., is useful.

A participle must be parsed twice: 1st, as a VERB in the "Participial Mood," (Allen and Cornwell,) a mood which admits a subject in *any* of the cases: 2ndly, as an ADJECTIVE, by the 2nd Concord. An adjective may be treated as follows, to save time. "*Ingenuas;* Fem. Pl. with *artes* (which is) accusative, after the Transitive *Didicisse,*" as object. To parse artes *again,* after this, would be a proof of *inattention.* "Artes; from ars, artis," is enough. *(These examples are from the Eton Grammar.*

Such answers as "Dative of Advantage"—"Ablative of the instrument," &c. are too vague.

"Magistro is Dative, because *giving the book* is an advantage to the *Master.*" "Jaculis is Ablative, because *darts* are instruments of *defence;*" and so forth.—These last answers substitute research for guessing. In each Lesson, a few *well chosen* words, with Deriv. and Key-words, may be parsed in writing, and a few more *vivâ voce, in full,* according to the "Samples" in p. 47, and without any questions from the Master; who can, afterwards, demand *precise* answers on *any* points requiring further notice.

N. B.—"*Perfect* Infinitive *Active*" is *not* the precise answer to "What *Mood* " is didicisse?

Qu. Why not treat the Greek Datives ποντῳ, Μουσαις, &c. as Dative OR Ablative, pro re natâ? [just like ponto, Musis, &c., in Latin.]

* These 3 "HELPS" are printed separately; for insertion, as fly-sheets, in any Grammar.

SYNTAX TABLE.

NAMES OF CASES.		SIGNS OF CASES.	ENGLISH TYPE OF LATIN CASES.
Nom.	1. BEFORE *any* Verb not Infinitive, as "Subject"	None	*He* speaks.
	2. AFTER "Esse & Co." when a Nominative precedes	None	This is *He.*
Acc.	1. AFTER a *Transitive* Verb, as "Object"	None	I saw *Him.*
	2. BEFORE *any* Verb Infinitive, as "Subject"	"That;" or none	I know *Him* to be (or, that He is) wise.
	3. AFTER "Esse & Co." when an Accusative precedes	None	I knew *it* to be *Him.*
	4. AFTER some Prepositions; expressed, or omitted	None wanted	*Him.*
Gen.	AFTER a former Noun; expressed, omitted, or *included* in some other word.....[*In Greek, after some Prepositions*]	Of, &c.	Of *Him;* or *His.*
Dat.	AFTER words denoting advantage or disadvantage	To, for, from, &c., or none	Give it to *Him;* or Give it *Him.*
Ablat.	1. Denoting the cause, means, or instrument, of an action or fact	Through, by, with, &c.	With darts, &c. (P)
	2. "Absolute;" with a Participle, of which it is the "Subject" [*In Greek, the Genitive, &c.*]	None	*He* being dead, they wept.
	3. AFTER Comparatives....[*In Greek, the Genitive.*]	"Than"	Than *He,* or than *Him.*
	4. AFTER some Prepositions; expressed, or omitted	None wanted	*Him.*
Voc.	Only used in addressing Persons	O; or none	*O Thou,* or *Thou.*

N.B.—The words "BEFORE" and "AFTER" refer only to the *English* place of the words; and are therefore very useful guides to the *Construing.*

SAMPLES OF PARSING, ADAPTED FOR ANY LANGUAGE.

The numeral column refers to the *Italic* portions of the following sentences :—

1. I behold *him.*
2. Vous le *respectez.*
3. *Imperat* pecunia.
4. Te *rediisse* gaudeo.
5. *Rerum* peritus.
6. *Patriæ* sit idoneus.
7 & 8. Æneas *tendens* palmas.
9. Imperante *Augusto.*

OBS.—In parsing one's own Language, *every* particular should be stated : but in a foreign or dead language, the previous Construing [which must never disagree with the Parsing] is supposed to have settled *what part of speech* each word is.

	VERB or NOUN, &c.	FROM	Voice.	Mood.	Tense. Gend.	No. No.	Person. Case.	REASON, OR RULE, OR BOTH.	DERIVATION OR DERIVATIVE. In any Languages.	KEYWORD. In any Languages.
1	Him	He, His, Pron. of 3rd Person	......	......	Mas.	Sing.	Accus.	AFTER the Transitive, "Behold," as Object. (Syntax Rule.)	ἑ, Ihn, Ihm.	?
2	Respect-ez	Respect-er -ant, -é.	Act.	Ind.	Pres.	Pl.	2nd.	Agreeing with Nom. Subject, "Vous." (Rule of Concord.)	Respectueux.	*Disrespect.*
3	Imper-at	-o -avi, -are, -atum	Act.	Ind.	Pres.	Sing.	3rd.	Agreeing with Nom. Subject, "Pecunia." (Concord.)	In & paro. (Freund.)	{ Imperative. *Empereur.*
4	Red-iisse	-eo,-ivi(-ii) -ire, -itum.	Act.	Inf.	Perf.	Sing.	2nd.	Agreeing with Accus. Subject, "Te." (Syntax Rule.)	Re & eo.	?
5	Rerum	Res, rei	......	......	Fem.	Pl.	Gen.	AFTER former Noun *Knowledge,* included in "Peritus."	χρεος χρημα ?	Real. *Rien.*
6	Patri-æ	-a, -æ	......	......	Fem.	Sing.	Dat.	Because his being "suitable," is an Advantage to his Country. (Rule for Dat.)	Pater.	Patriot.
7	Tend-ens	-o, tetendi, -ere, ten- -tum(sum)	Act.	Part.	Pres.	Sing.	3rd.	Agreeing with Nom. Subject, "Æneas." (Concord of Verb.)	τεινω.	{ Tendency. Subtense. Contention.
8	Tend-ens	-entis	......	......	Mas.	Sing.	Nom.	Agreeing with Noun, *Æneas.* (Conc. of Adj.	{ Augeo. Aête.	August. *Août.*
9	August-o	-us, -i	......	......	Mas.	Sing.	Abl.	*Æneas,* as subject. Absolute, BEFORE Imperante.		

To be written on Blank Forms, with any *intelligible* abbreviations, such as *A.* for "AFTER ;" *B.* for "BEFORE ;" *a. f. n.* for "after former noun ;" *Ag. w.* for "Agreeing with," &c.

HELPS TO "CONSTRUING."

From the very first, in declining Nouns, call Musa "song," "*a* song," "*the* song," *by turns;* or, for practice, *all* 3 *at once.* Distinguish the Nom. and Acc. thus:— " Nom. lapis, a stone, *subject;*" " Acc. lapidem, a stone, *object.*" When you join Hic. hæc, hoc, with a noun, give it its true meaning;—as, " Hic lapis, *this* stone ;" and now and then try " *Ille* lapis, *that* stone;" " Qui lapis, *which* stone ;" and so on, all through.

Indulge, at times, *every* case of *every* Adjective with 3 terminations, though they ⎱ felicem, felicem, felix. may be exactly alike, *e.g.* ⎰ felicibus, felicibus, felicibus. But also, take care to be ABLE to say them, and every thing else, in *all* the ways in which they ever have been said (at *least*); adding, in Greek, " Abl τη τιμη, *with* the honour," after the Vocative. Decline Amavi twice over: 1st, as "I have loved," (Perfect ;) 2nd, "I loved or did love," (Aorist.) Avoid " *can*" and " *could*" as signs of Tenses, and consider " Possum amare" as the truest Potential of Amo. Say the Subjunctive, *with* conjunctions ut, ne, si, &c., and Amarem and Amavissem also separately, as a *Conditional* Mood. When you come to make out SENTENCES, the ORDER is the first difficulty. Look at this Syntax Table *thoughtfully*, and you will find it also a *Construing* as well as Parsing Table ;—for the words BEFORE and AFTER will set you right in " taking" so many of the words, that the rest can hardly choose but fall into their places of themselves. Then, as to *grouping :* begin with taking *every* word by itself, and *never* join two without knowing *why.* You will soon see that a *preposition, with its noun,* is no more than *a case;* for—

e. g.: Ad Caium, } to Caius,   Per timorem, } through fear;
           Caio,   }   Timore,   }

so that you may safely join *them*. Next, the epithet-adjective
is a plant too feeble to stand alone for a moment, [the *"*Enw
gwan*," of Welsh grammar,] and must needs cling, like a
tendril, to its Noun; thus, Bonus puer, a good boy. So
the adverb to the Verb,—Benè scribere, to write well.
But sometimes the Adjective *tells us news* (Predicate), and
deserves to be taken separately.   Puer, the boy—est, is—
bonus, good.   And the Adverb now and then is too weighty
to be merged with its great partner.   See also above,
" Soracte," &c.   * *(= weak noun.)*

A Pronoun Subject, with its auxiliaries and Participle,
forming a " Compound Tense ;" as, " J' aurais eu," " Ich
würde gehabt haben," being equivalent to the single word
habuissem, may be grouped, *for that reason*, (compare the
case of Preposition with Noun).   So may, perhaps, *any*
number of words, when they either represent a single one
in the other language, or constitute an actual " *Phrase.*"

The less obvious cases, and " open questions," will, to
the very last, form an instructive exercise of judgment and
taste.   But, for your Conjunction, you will *never* find a
suitable partner : he is a confirmed old bachelor.   It is true
that Que and its *word* are great friends in *Latin :* but that
is no rule for John Bull,—" Nolumus leges Angliæ mutari."
Besides, the *in*-separable que of quisque, plerumque, &c.,
requires a contrast.   Therefore, say, " Arma, arms—que,
and—virum, the Man;" as we lads did on the banks of
Sabrina.—" κὰι γενοὶ αν ὸυ κακος."

HELPS TO COMPOSITION.
(Especially Latin.)

THE Verb, that ponderous element, naturally finds its
way, by specific gravity, to the very bottom of the sen-

tence or clause. On the same principle, so to speak, the governing words are generally found *below* the governed. This goes a good way towards arranging the general framework of an average sentence. But—carefully observe and study, in the best prose writers, the *local* value of words, and the laws of EMPHASIS,—the best key to most glaring Exceptions. The *place* of negatives, as non, οὐκ, οὐδὲ, ne—quidem, &c.; and of et, καὶ, quoque, &c. [compared with ne pas, nicht, même, auch, &c.] will furnish good illustrations of "local value." Relative clauses [in Greek very often replaced by the Article and Participle, ὁ πιστευων] are generally quasi-parenthetic. As in *words*, so in *sentences*, EUPHONY has its claims, and induces aberrant order within certain limits, the settlement of which is the province of discrimination and an *educated Ear*. And, in versification, the question of Sound *versus* Sense is still more extensive and refined. See p. 55.

For the detail, in prose and verse, *vide* omninò virum desideratissimum.--T. K. ARNOLD.

END OF THE HELPS.

———

LANGUAGES AND LANGUAGE.

SOME people seem to study Languages, one after the other, and yet never to acquire or even seek any knowledge of Language,—its nature, history, laws, changes, constitution, *diseases*, accidents, &c., any of which might afford subject of consideration and research for one's life long; even as others make the acquaintance of a host of individuals in the vegetable world, without any definite idea of the real nature of a *plant* as such, its structure, functions, or purpose in the economy of nature. This, however, is the more inexcusable in the instance first mentioned, inasmuch as the subject-matter is perpetually, not only in our hands but even in our very mouths; which, in botanical specimens, is only the case with that limited class which are either carried about as ornaments (des bouquets), or dressed in and for another sense (des legumes). Words are not only for ever passing the ivory and coral barriers of the "human face divine," ἔρκος ὀδόντων, but gentlemen, and even fayre ladyes, are sometimes forced to eat them! Then the most unreflecting amongst us are occasionally induced to become ruminants; a process which, if it includes the act of reasoning, can not, in the judgment of the late logician, Archbishop Whately, be carried on without the instrumentality of winged words—ἔπεα πτεροεντα. They constitute a currency: we coin them, and if passable they pass. And yet, though we use and abuse them, either aloud or tacitly, in more ways than I have time to think, much less to write of, yet there are many who never bestowed a thought on them, but became proficients in their own and one or two other languages without being able to give any distinct account what language is in itself,—how it differs from a tune on the bag-pipes, the bellowing of a bull, or the eternal clack of a mill, each of which have their analogues in human speech. Now, to pass over a host of deeply interesting particulars in the Philosophy of Language, one important purpose in studying other tongues besides our own, is that of gleaning from the materials thus presented to us those excellencies which help to frame a beau ideal of a language more perfect that any of the existing ones, and out of which any of them might help themselves with benefit, till it may please God to remove the Babel difficulty, and make the earth once more of one speech—a monoglot world.* It is disheartening to a teacher who knows the

---

* Query—Do the pious followers of Mr. D. H. hope to get rid of *all* languages, and substitute their *far more convenient and precise* ʀᴀᴘs? "Di meliora piis!"

value of Comparative Philology, to find how little encouragement is given to tuition that aims at any thing beyond the utilitarian acquisition of words and phrases. I strongly suspect that if Max Müller himself were a family tutor, and the children told their Papa that he was teaching them language instead of languages, he would in most cases be dismissed: on le chasserait sur le champ! Now, if the judgment is worth cultivating, I think one very strong reason for studying spoken languages, as French and German, is that we may compare their respective merits as vehicles of thought; and enquire, 1st, which of them has the best stock, the most expressive assortment of names and verbs to make use of; the best set of moods, tenses, and auxiliaries, of cases and prepositions, to modify that assortment; and, 2nd, which nation *makes the best use* of their existing materials. To illustrate such an investigation as this:—We find the Germans possessed of a single past tense or Aorist, which has to do the double duty of Aorist and Imperfect, so that it is impossible to know, except from the context, whether ich schrieb means I *wrote* the letter, or *was writing* it. Here is a want of materials to work with; and the only question is whether they might not borrow a hint from their children the English, who would now say, Gideon *was threshing* wheat, instead of *threshed*, and thereby gain in precision. Not having a tense corresponding with j'ecriverai, they do condescend to manufacture a compound tense, ich werde schreiben. So, since they are equally at a loss for an equivalent to J'ecrivais, why not stoop to the use of a periphrastic form, ich war schreibend? just as the English have, *on second thoughts;* and no one *now* thinks "I was writing," awkward or round-about, though perhaps at first it seemed so. This, however, is Mein Herr's difficulty. Let us next look into Monsieur's petites affaires. He has a remarkably fine Aorist, J'ecrivis,— is,— it, as well as the aforesaid Imperfect J'ecrivais,— ais,— ait, and is beautifully precise in the use of them, where a German would have no choice. But then in another case, viz., that of Aorist versùs Perfect, the French perpetrate a most barbarous and wanton confusion.

I take the following example from Le Page's useful school-book, " L'Echo de Paris," p. 6, 34th edition :—" Nous *avons* été à la peche. *Avez vous* été heureux ? *Nous avons* pris un brochet. *Est* c' à la ligne que vous l'*avez* pris ?" If this be translated into English, Greek, or German, *precisely*, " We have been a-fishing. Have you been fortunate ? We have caught a pike. Is it with a line you have caught him ?" we should, in all three languages, understand the fishing to have occurred *on that same day.* And, you will ask, does not the French equally lead us to think so ? Undoubtedly ; as I have quoted it, it could suggest no other idea; but I have purposely omitted the key to my objection. The first of the above sentences actually stands, " Nous avons été à la peche *jeudi dernier.*" Try this in the other languages ; and in any of them, not only the *words*, " I *have* been a-fishing *last Thursday*," will be improper, but the *idea* itself is equally incorrect. That is, the French, when they have it in their power to say "Nous *fumes* a la peche jeudi dernier," and thus express the Aorist *idea* by an Aorist *tense*, " I *was* a-fishing last Thursday," *prefer* a tense which can only represent that idea by a defiance of the universally received and philosophically true definition of that tense. I know not whether Clarke's explanation of tenses is original, but it was in his Homer (Iliad I. 37, Notes) that I first saw them classed rationally.

NONSENSE VERSES.

BESIDES the large class who see no good in troubling
one's head with languages that no one ever thinks of speaking nowadays—(" and what else," say they, " is language
good for ?") there is another, outside of that, who would
confine classical reading to the prose writers, the pedestrians
of Greece and Rome ; and leave the poetry, because "if you
want *that*, there is nothing like our own Milton and Shaks-
peare, you know :" and another class outside that again,
who have no objection to the study of those great masters
of rhythm, and melody, and high conception, but can see
no use in bothering lads with *making bad Greek and
Latin verses of their own.* Lastly, and external to all these,
there are a set of sages, who say, let boys learn to make
verses by all means ; first bad ones, then better, and at last
good ones ; but why spend time over *nonsense* verses ? I'll
tell you, my time-saving friends, if you can spare me a little
of your own time for my nonsense prose, (and cons; a pun lost
upon some readers in a previous work, so I repeat it delibe-
rately : " ambell lab," ye ken, " tyr y garreg," ye ken, see p.
75). But before I deal with this last Company, (limited,) let
me tell *all* the classes above specified, that, if they expect all
their children to be *good English* scholars, (without miracle,)
they should get them taught some Greek and Latin, and
taught them *well* too. Next, if they wish them to be classical
scholars, they never will be so without the poets. If they
wish to appreciate the beauties of these poets, they must *try*
to imitate their beauties, whether they succeed tolerably, or
fail miserably. Finally, if they wish to make verses *at all*,
they ought to *begin* with nonsense verses, and keep at that
work (or diversion ?) till they can make very good ones
indeed—better, I should say, than any sense verses that

ever were seen. Why so? Because, first of all, metre is a
separate study, as distinct from every other branch as the
Eton prosody is from the accidence and syntax; the metre
is not only distinct from the sense, but the two may be
almost considered as natural enemies; at any rate, the
scholar will find, from first to last, a constant fight between
the two, sometimes a deadly struggle, as the expressions
" repugnante metro," " Triclinius metrum pessundat," &c.,
loudly testify. Nor is the subject a very easy one, when one
considers that in a common hexameter the syllables vary
from 17 to 13, and in a pentameter from 14 to 12, whilst
the succession of feet passes through a vast range of permu-
tations and combinations. It is, therefore, mere humanity,
the negation of cruelty to animals, in accordance with
Martin of Galway's humane act, not to trouble the lad's
brain with the two subjects at once, the sense *and* the metre,
but to let him bestow his time on the construction of poetry
that will " scan," without construing, till he is quite familiar
with the form of the verses, and can makè them " scan and
prove," as a matter of course. Then, having broken the
neck of one great difficulty, he sets about translating, from
Bland, Rapier, Oxenham, &c., easy English into Latin, *pre-
disposed* to fall into a shape which is already familiar to
him from practice, and of which, as a question of feet and
cæsura, he thoroughly knows the value. Fancy the luxury
of this, compared with the heartless drudgery of squeezing
words into a mould, the exact nature of which has to be
ascertained (or rather enquired after) each time; and the
result of which, after all, the poor fellow just *hopes* will scan
and construe, being only almost half sure of the latter! I
would therefore, inculcate, as "an elder soldier," upon those
who teach verses at all, to insist upon a degree of perfection
in the *un*meaning lines, which the stern requisitions of

meaning sometimes render so difficult that we hear " necessitas ineluctabilis " pleaded for liberties which the *less* stern laws of even Greek prosody have forbidden. I say " less stern " for we find the Roman poet Martial felicitating the Greeks on the laxity of *their* metrical rules, compared with the unbending muse of Italy. " Felices Graii—queis Α'ρες Α'ρες licet sonare." Finally, young fellow teachers, my brother chips and sister shavings of the scholastic profession, I advise you not only to adhere to the good old practice of nonsense verses in spite of the ridicule which is so easily cast upon this and many other really practical subjects, but to commence it *much earlier* than it is ordinarily introduced; and further, to try prosody (as I did at Bristol College, I think with good effect) in prose as well as poetry ; and make your pupils scan and prove the words of Cæsar as well as the feet of Virgil, and learn the declensions and conjunctions from the first with *a special view* to the requirements of verse composition in after life—a point which that old foe and friend of my childhood, the Fleur de Lis or Eton grammar, evidently did not overlook either in the prose Accidentia or in those " remarkable poems," Propria quæ Maribus and As in præsenti. *(" Dulce est desipere, in loco.")*

SPECIAL AND GENERAL TRAINING.

Suppose, as an experiment, two boys, A and B, brought up as follows, both being intended for the same employment in after life :—A is taught those branches only which are of immediate use to him in his business, and which he will have to carry on *personally* after he leaves school. Any thing that there is an option of laying aside is omitted, as being *practically* useless for his special vocation. B learns every thing that is generally useful; avoiding *all* that pertains peculiarly to his intended calling: nothing is attempted but the improvement of his intellectual faculties; he is fitted for thinking and acting judiciously in general on occasions that may present themselves; but the particular occasions that inevitably *will* arise in his profession are purposely left blank for the present. Of course each of these lads gets a defective education, and is under opposite disadvantages. But it is an interesting question to consider how their several conditions would tell upon their future career. I can imagine them as follows:—A would be an adept at his work from the very first; and, having acquired no taste for intellectual improvement, would consider his education finished, and his leisure hours due to amusements; whilst "slow coaches" in the same office would have a good deal to learn in order to get through their daily tasks with credit. Still he *may* escape the snares of idleness and vice, and, by his expert business-like habits, get into an office of his own before the average period. Here he will come into contact with a variety of minds and circumstances which it is his business to discern and to control; perplexing questions, physical, moral, or social, may naturally arise, with an important indirect bearing upon his prospects. His powers of observation, reflection, judgment, &c., may be taxed to the utmost to meet emergencies. *Natural* shrewdness and tact *may* bring him through cleverly; but, *that is not to our present purpose;* his boyish *education* has furnished no *aid* for triumphs of this kind. *That* taught him nothing beyond the dexterous performance of technicalities in a subordinate position, where he had all ready to his hand. It has given him no *master*-mind to foresee, modify, or weather the storms of life. B of course finds himself awkward at a novel occupation; but then his whole training has been a successful struggle

with the difficulties of language and science, and he is prepared to cope with those minor perplexities of any other
subject which only stimulate his pugnacity to win fresh
laurels.   Mental superiority soon places him above those
who at first laughed at his awkwardness in technical
details; and they shortly see him "at the top of the tree."
But it is in his subsequent career, as Principal, that his
advantages come into full view.   There, his perspicacious
and comprehensive mind grasps with equal facility the
minute and the vast in his professional questions; and
whilst the mere drudge is calculating results, he foresees,
avoids, or turns them to account.

Such is, *on paper*, the difference between A and B!   I
would follow it up with other cases, but I feel too much
sympathy with the next two worthies, C, D, after a recent
illness, and must rest a little.—(*Sept.*, 1863.)

CLASSICAL EXPERIENCE.

AT a very early age, when rummaging amongst a heap of
loose books, I met with a very strange-looking one, in an
unknown tongue, and bound in a very coarse greenish-yellow
buckram.   The title page bore an escutcheon with a most
ferocious looking animal, (which I afterwards learnt was
Felis Leo,) and three fleur de lis.   Below all this stood the
venerable names of Pote and Williams.   Full of laudable
curiosity, which my dear parents ever rejoiced to gratify, I
ran to my father to ask what it was.   I found him in the
old dining room; I mean *the* original room where the rats'
white feet used to show under the skirting-board, before he
and his indulgent landlord had indulged *each other* (?) with
the *de*formation and *re*formation of that quaint red brick

mansion with steep slate roof,—prominent garret windows,
—and a high flight of stone steps—few of the like now left
in North Wales, G. R. Query—Does Cornis, near Flint, retain its old form?   Well, there I found him with a few
friends,—perhaps the said Landlord, perhaps Col. Lloyd of
Marle, perhaps James Royle, but *most certainly* " Parry of
Glanydon," Clerk, whose top boots and limp I can not mistake at this distance (time = space, ye ken), and there they
sat, I believe discussing Raikes' Port with walnuts off the
tree on the left, and Swan Eggs off the pear tree on the
right—to this day in statu quo, are they not?   I broke in
upon their quiet little quorum (no unwelcome intruder,
albeit at times abrupt, and the bearer of queer messages
from the Hwsmon or Dairy-maid) with the anxious enquiry,
" Father, what book is this?"   He had kept up Latin
enough to recognise his old acquaintance, longo post tempore
visum, and at once told me it was a Latin Grammar ; adding
an envoi which all the ups and downs of life could never
efface, " and mind, Johnnie, you must have every word of
this at your finger ends by-and-by."   I looked aghast at the
outlandish pages of " Quæ genus," " As in præsenti," &c.   I
believe I would have bitten those little finger ends *off* rather
than furnish them with such abominations ; and, after the
usual questions by neighbour Parry " whether I was to be
Lord Chancellor or Archbishop of Canterbury," &c., I made
my escape, a sadder and a wiser man than I came in !
Without losing a moment, I stuffed the thin little book (an
Eton Accidence) as far as I could drive it under the promiscuous pile on the lobby floor ; without a shadow of suspicion
that there was another like it in the wide world, and pretty
sure that *that* one would never be brought to light to plague
me withal.   Heu spes necquicquam dulces !   By the aid of
my earliest and dearest friend, W. L., who used to spend

his holidays either at Pwllycrochon, or at " Old Evans', of Colwyn," this green dragon of a book was ferreted out, and in a few years, *i.e.,* before I went to Halton's at ten, most of it *was* exactly where my Father had predicted. Q. E. F. But in the meantime, I was imperceptibly undergoing a training still more valuable than " Propria quæ maribus." I had imbibed Welsh quasi cum nutricis lacte, and was taught English expressly, besides the constant use of it in the family, my step-sisters being half English and knowing that language far better of the two. Thus, like many Welsh children, I became an early proficient in two languages; a very important intellectual advantage, which may help to account for our acknowledged superiority, *cæteris paribus,* to our neighbours, the "Saxon porkers" of Ivanhoe. But I had, in addition to this, a special leading to philological enquiry; my father frequently had intercourse with his rustic neighbours, workmen, &c., in the presence of English visitors, to whom he had to interpret the conversation; and he would sometimes call their attention, with honest pride, to the beauty and force of our Celtic idioms, and the difficulty of doing them justice in *their* lingo. This naturally led me to notice such facts for myself, and to question others. I was also present at justice business; which, from intimate knowledge of the parties, plaintiff and defendant, and the oddity of their complaints and excuses, was intensely amusing to an inquisitive urchin. Robert Edwards, of Groes, Shopkeeper, could swear conscientiously that John Hughes the Clerk's wife, had put him in bodily fear; which diverted me exceedingly for years, coupled with his placid, handsome, *Jewish,* but somewhat sickly features, to which her *most Christian* majesty's bold bearing presented a striking contrast. Again, Cadi Siôn Emawnt (Ang. John Edmond's daughter Katie) laid a complaint against Siôn Swch and Siân his wife, for witholding just wages; a charge which led to a nice discrimination between " gwas'naethu," regular *hired* service, and " gweithio" working (however long and hard) *without* definite arrangement by high contracting parties. To all these discussions the embryo Slickensides would " seriously incline." And, as His Majesty's Justices of the Quorum made all their remarks on the evidence in English, a good deal of Comparative Grammar was there also drawn out, for the instruction of the egîn ysgolhaig. With these immense advantages (as I now know them to be) it was no wonder that I rather startled them at Chester by the ease with which I mastered Valpy's Delectus (no better book has replaced it), after a little help from my flexible class-fellow John Grace ; and that my master, J. Halton, was chagrined at his Captain's removal to a neighbouring school kept by W. Fish, which he justly considered *not so very much* superior to his own. Having added Latin verses and Greek grammar, at Stanley Place, to the good old-fashioned " grounding" I got at The Bars, I passed a fair examination in Dr. Butler's study, and was at once placed in the " Shell" of Shrewsbury School, then by far the best in England ; where I was passing upwards to the top of the tree, only for one Benjamin H. Kennedy, (now the Head in the highest sense,) beating me as he beat everybody and everything else, and leaving me the sufficient honour of remaining a *respectable* second to *such* a first, till we parted, soon to meet again at Cambridge, to work in the same relative position to the goal. Proximus huic, quanto sed proximus intervallo ! What " him and me," and our school-fellows accomplished in those days, may be seen in the Oxford and Cambridge Calendars. What Salopians are doing *now*-a days, in ditto, ditto, and in many fields of competition that have since been opened, " in usum studiosæ juventutis." [For both, see Sabrinæ Corolla.] I advise those who aim at the like *Philological* distinctions, to beware of a Welsh, Irish, or Gaelic competitor, who has been accustomed to two languages from infancy. Er mag wohl Doppelkopf heissen. "Deuben ydyw Robin !" Ye Celts, learn English; but also, *hold your own*, tooth and nail!

REMARKS ON THUCYDIDES, ii. 65.

THE chapter concludes with the following words : Τοσουτον Περικλεῖ ἐπερίσσευσε τότε ἀφ' ὧν αὐτὸς προέγνω καὶ πάνυ ἂν ῥᾳδίως περιγενέσθαι τῶν Πελομοννησιων αὐτῶν τῷ πολέμῳ. " This remarkable phrase," as Bloomfield rightly calls it, has met with a charming reception (since "variety is charming ") at the hands of the critics. I. Gottleber says, " Tantum præstabat reliquis tunc temporis ingenio Pericles, quo adjutus res futuras ante capiebat. Tantum tum Pericles cæteros superabat, *ob id quod* ipse prævidebat facile civitatem Peloponnesiis solis superiorem bello fore." II. Göller says, " Tantum superabat (virium) Pericli ad Peloponnesios solos iis quæ ipse præviderat atque facillime quidem in hoc bello devincendos." III. Gail favours us with, " Tant s'etait montré superieur dans ses calculs le génie de Pericles, qui avait prévu que dans cette guerre du Peloponnèse la république se soutiendrait même sans effort." IV. Bloomfield himself quotes Portus and Hobbes for rendering it, " Such was the depth of judgment displayed by Pericles, whereby he foresaw that they might easily frustrate all the efforts of the Peloponnesians in the war." And he further proposes to supply the ellipse by the abundant *(sagacity)* of Pericles *(respecting those measures)* by which he foresaw," &c. V. Arnold gives, " Such a superabundance of means did Pericles then possess, from which he of himself foresaw (or judged beforehand) that with the utmost ease he could triumph over the mere unaided force of the Peloponnesians. So much *more* than enough had he to encounter the Peloponnesians, since there was almost enough to contend successfully with the united force of the Peloponnesians, Sicily, and Persia . . ." Cæteraque gravissimè.

It is needless to enter minutely into the respective merits of these various renderings. Some of them treat τότε, αὐτὸς, and αὐτῶν as insignificant little words. One refers ἐπερίσσευσε to the superiority of Pericles' genius; another to the resources of the Republic in his days; ἀφ' ὧν, is by one supposed to mean the " measures by which ;" by another, the " means from which " the Peloponnesians were to be conquered; by a third, "the sagacity " by which Pericles foresaw their easy conquest; and one boldly translates it " *ob id quod ;*" not to mention Göller's still more daring flight.

I strongly suspect the poor little truth has escaped amid the confusion; and that the superabundance alluded to by Thucydides was not an excess of wit, of means, or of measures, but of *data* or *grounds* for Pericles' opinion. If so, the meaning will be, " So ample, nay, *more* than ample, were, at that time, the grounds on which the master-mind of Pericles predicted the easy conquest of the Peloponnesians single-handed." More literally, " So much was-there-over-and-above then to Pericles (of grounds) from which he (of) himself prejudged that they would even easily conquer the Peloponnesians (by) themselves." Pericles had *more* than sufficient data for his inference, had the Peloponnesians been the *sole* opponents, since he was not so very wrong even when they had so many auxiliaries. He must have been *super*abundantly furnished with correct premises at first, (τότε) seeing that, even with so serious an alteration of those premisses afterwards, yet his prediction was not falsified for three years.

If I do not mistake, Dr. Arnold *alone* has given the true sense of ἐπερίσσευσε, whilst *he* too has erred in supposing the antecedent of ἀφ᾽ ὧν, to be the *physical* resources of the Republic for conquering the Peloponnesians, instead of the *mental* resources (*i.e.*, data, premisses, or grounds,) of Pericles for inferring their easy conquest. Syntactically, the question is whether ἀφ᾽ ὧν belongs to προεγνω, or to περιγενέσθαι ; my proposal of course supposes it connected with προέγνω.

HOMER A SCREW.

(Not generally known.)

AN author's character may often be inferred, with more or less certainty, from little traits which escape unawares to himself, and by which he may therefore be said, with the greatest propriety, to be *be-trayed*. Old Homer appears to me to have made a slip of this kind, in the charming story of Glaucus and Diomedes, which many of my readers must have read, either in Greek or English, or both, with great pleasure. It is so much the fashion now-a-days to translate Homer, that I have half a mind to indulge the honest John Bull correspondent whom I answered rather tartly in No. 3, p. 102,* with a slice of *the* Greek Poet in the vulgar tongue. The passage is one beautifully illustrative of the early existence of that spirit of chivalry by which man, even in the savage circumstances of a sanguinary slaughter-field, manifests the under-current of a relatively better though deeply fallen nature ; and would have the bystanders and after-readers to know that, even in the most brutal of all corporate transactions—WAR, he

* Of " *Old Price's Remains*," 1863–4.

is, after all, *not* a gorilla. The scene is one of great ten-
derness and simplicity; and it is highly refreshing, after
plunging through the terrific Inkermannish shindies where
this eminent *Old Bird* (Mæonii carminis alès.—*Hor.*) has,
with chirurgical coolness and precision, been making his
heroes hack, hew, and perforate the frontals, sternals,
humerals, and abdominals of their adversaries, to drop
upon such an episode as this, where two representative men
of the dauntless aggressors and defenders of Troy town
volunteer a parley (without the "bottle-holding" interven-
tion of a Secretary for Foreign Affairs,) and actually, for
a brief space, manage, even in those days and at such a time,
to talk and behave like gentlemen, aye, like honourable
gentlemen of the House of Commons, if they do not equal
in courtesy the noble occupants of "an other place" *convay-
nient.* " Ut recté notavit Eustathius, ὁ ποιητης ἀνιησι το τοῦ
πολεμου ἀκμαιον, και ἀναπανει τον ἀκροατην." The ame-
nities of their gracious interview are at last appropriately
clenched by an act highly significant of the moral difference
between πολεμιος and ἐχθρος, as afterwards between *hostis*
and *inimicus.* They exchange armour, as peers of the
realm of physical and moral might; and, as such, naturally
waive all regard to intrinsic value. Not so our poet. After
declaring, roundly, that poor Glaucus must have been bereft
of his senses, (the subject of what we should now call
"judicial blindness,") to consent to "swop even hands,"—he
first notices, with care, the widely different materials of
which the Greek and Trojan suits were respectively composed, viz., "χαλκεα χρυσειων," brazen for golden; and
then, not content with this, the *Old Screw,* the *dear,* but
horrid Old Screw, must need calculate, coldly and commer-
cially, the precise *pecu*niary value (*i.e.*, the value in *cows,*)
of the two "articles" in question; and so "closes his

account" with two epithets which, however sonorously he or the itinerant rhapsodists may have delivered them, yet possess no more intrinsic dignity than the humble "hapurth" of an English small-ware shop. Ἑκατομβοὶ ἐννεαβοιων! quoth Mæonides; which pair of high-sounding words, thunder them out as you will, convey no feeling more elevated than, maybe, fresh amazement at the strange fact that Glaucus should have been such a goose as to give the value of 100 head of beeves in exchange for that of 9: a clear loss of 91 per cent.! I always picture to myself the venerable Scald—(of Chios, or which of those other six candidate cities who pulled caps for the honour of producing him?) pausing after the recitation of that financial line, and whispering to himself, with uplifted eyes, "νηπιος! νηπιος"! It reminds me of the niggardly spirit in which Judas Iscariot grumbles at the extravagance of that woman of blessed memory. "Why was not this ointment sold for 300 pence, and given to the poor?" Thy dirty pence perish with thee, Judas! a murrain on thy skinny cows, Homer!

A TRAGIC TALE.

Communicated in confidence to the Poet, by a Skeleton not in Armour.
(See a real Poem by Longfellow.)
"Κτεινω δε τους ξυμπαντας."—Œd. Tyr.
Dedicated to my 21 Nephews and Nieces in general, but to C. and F. W.
in particular.

I say, Skinny, says the Bard,
Don't you think it rather hard
You should keep, in that strange way,
At a fellow, night and day?

Ans.—"To be an Uncle was my greatest fear;

¹"So I killed my brother and three sisters dear;
"And here ²I am: the sod on ²me lies ³heavy—
"But—I never had a Niece, nor yet a Nevvy!"
Here to the word he suited well the action,
Rubbing his bony hands with satisfaction.
More had he told me, but, says I, "enough!"
I hadn't patience with such horrid stuff!

NOTES—1. Of course it was *very wrong of him;* but, apart from the morality of the case, perhaps a more *effectual* method could not have been substituted. We all know (we Uncles especially), that " prevention is better than cure ;" and, with deceased's idiosyncrasy, any other plan might have led to a far greater sacrifice of human life.

2. *"I"* and *"me."* It is an interesting feature in Psychology, that this confusion of the subjective is met with in other cases of *ghost-craft* and *ghost-lore.* Poor Old Homer does not reach the fifth line without getting into a mess. He says Πολλους δ' ἰφθιμους ψυχας Αῖδι προιαψεν Η'ρωων· αὐτους δε ἑλωρια τευχε κυνεσσιν. Just fancy—αὐτους! as if the poor carcase—the "insepulta membra" that go " ἐς κορακας ὄντως" were one's proper *self*, rather than the "valiant soul," which he has just consigned to Hades. In Virgil, the shade of Palinurus, that best of pilots, yet does not *steer* clear of *this* danger. After a grand description of such a " cropper," as none but this dozing old Tar ever experienced, (Æn. vi. 349—351) he not only identifies his present naked self with the *late* Palinurus, a living soul clothed with flesh and bones, but, after describing his own violent death by the hands of mistaken wreckers, he *persists* in saying " Nunc *me* fluctus habet, versantque in littore venti." I hope these metaphysical *scrapes* will have an interest for some readers who, like myself, *had not common patience* with a man so averse to the trials of Uncleship that he is reported to have said " He'd *hang* first," and to have been *"as good as his word."* And what of Horace ? Is *he* altogether guiltless of jumblement in Book i. Od. 28, where the ghost of Archytas implores a Jack Tar, in formâ pauperis, to come "down with his dust," on the hackneyed ground that "his honour would not be any poorer?" Read the Ode, (I have no time, E. R. to translate that *and* the Homer, if either) and you will see that this shady Dramatis Persona, though evidently μετεωρos or "afloat," says " *me* quoque devexi rapidus comes Orionis Illyricis notus obruit undis"

ON THE TENDENCY OF EVIL TO PERPETUATE ITSELF.

A Parody for the times, by a much put-about, and more pushed-about
Layman, *November and December*, 1863.

Martial wrote as follows :—

> Semper *eris* pauper, si pauper *es*, Æmiliane ;
> Dantur opes nulli nunc, nisi divitibus !

Our Author writes :—

> Semper *eris* claudus, si claudus *es*, Æmiliane ;
> Fit via vi nulli nunc, nisi præpetibus.

—and that too after talking in the Pythagorean strain—"nihil ultra nervos atque cutem morti concesserat atræ." In fact, it would be no easy matter for a writer of *any* creed to make a disembodied spirit talk *quite* consistently on all occasions : and accordingly you may notice that our modern spiritualists, who listen in *rapping* and *wrapt* attention to departed parties, allow a wide margin for scotographical errors ; and strongly insist upon it that we must *expect* these good souls to " blunder on" even in the other world ! So thought Virgil, Æn. vi. 736, " Quin et, supremo cum lumine vita reliquit, Non tamen *omne* malum miseris nec funditus *omnes* corporeæ excedunt pestes," &c.   But then *he* (very wisely) has arranged ample premises, with appropriate "plant" and machinery, where these "soiled copies" (of *post*-humous remains?) are washed, bleached, and hot-pressed before they have permission " supera ut convexa revisant," instead of allowing them the unenviable privilege of " coming again" in the rough, to expose their ignorance.   Truly My Lord Peter may hold his sides with laughing at Jack and Martin (see *Tale of a Tub*) if they abuse their liberty by running into such super-ultra-montanist vagaries ! O that *all three* would have done with their curious arts, bring their books together, burn them before all men (with or without counting the cost), and read their Bibles together by the light of that glorious bonfire ! "Trojaque nunc stares !"   What, says Old Tom, burn all the *good* religious books ? Yes, and welcome ; for the sake of getting rid of ALL the bad ones, and making a fresh start with *the* one book.

3.   Cf. " sit tibi terra levis," &c.

Free translation :—

> If you *are* lame, Old Fellow, lame you'll *stay* :
> Only for *fast* men now they " clear the way."

See the Song, Dic Sion Dafydd, *by Jack of Glan-y-gors.*

GENUS HOMO.

SINCE recent theories (and old ditto "new revived") have called our specific character in question, it is incumbent on us to look after and stick up for our *varieties,* (respecting the existence of which there is no controversy,) and reduce them to something like a scientific arrangement. The data for such a classification will be found both ample and possessed of an interest not inferior to that attached to *Species* recognised as such. Besides which, there is an element, all but peculiar to anthropology, which imparts a life to this study scarcely known in other departments of the Regne Animal. It arises from the fact that, in some varieties of the creature Homo, the females are distinguished from the males by traits of character si prononcès et tranchants, that it is impossible to refuse to them a separate place, and nomenclature. The glow-worm does not differ from its mate more decidedly than our own Evidæ (to give a name and place at once—we make short work at Νεφελοκοκκυγια) differ from the Adamidæ, so to be respectively designated henceforward. We subjoin a list of some of the leading varieties, with their British or Foreign synonymes :—1. Homo pauper diabolus ; Le Pauvre diable ; Der Blutarm ; [LE GUEUX *Berangeri*] ; *Tergo exili, glaberrimo : loculis nullis, aut plane vacuis ; " Corde levi, braccis tenuibus ;" " Consertum tegumen spinis, at cætera Graius." (Often hardly distinguishable from the next*

variety.) 2. H. Bonus diabolus; Le bon diable; probably
a -French var. of H. bonus *homo,* Le Bonhomme. 3. H.
femella improtecta, *described by Charivarius and figured
by Leech.* 4. H. sagax (H. providus; H. rationis particeps;)
Le Sage; The Sage; *Cerebro integro,* (rare.) 5. H. circin-
ata; La Crinolineè, *Spatiosa, rotundissima; pedibus
liberis, cubitis impeditiusculis: incessu propè divino,*
"*nec vox hominem sonat:*" *corpore imprimis combustibili;
(super-abundant in promenades, pumprooms, rows, &c.)*

Occasional specimens occur which, though not devoid of
individual interest, yet, can hardly be depended on as "per-
manent vanities;" whilst others are evidently local, or depen-
dent on age, climate, periodic moulting, or change of food;
but, as some of these elements lead ultimately to the establishment of the most marked characters, such cases as the
following may be recommended to further observation:—
H. nomistacus; H. Sanctigilesianus; H. baracawsius; H.
porcpiana; H. hasbeenia; H. discountus Cruikshankii.

The above remarks do not, however, apply to the next
set; unless, "H. nodiceps" has been hastily adopted.

H. pegleggatus:—the Timbertoe; *Crure dextro fraxineo,
sinistroossi-carneo;* (aliquando reversè) *rariùs ambobus
arborescentibus, (habitat, Greenwich and Chelsea.)* H. pig-
tailosus:—Crinibus occipitalibus contortuplicatis; anterio-
ribus, (ubi adsunt) liberis. [An extinct variety: Old Sir
Robt. Vaughan and *the* tall old man on St. George's Pierhead,
Liverpool, were the last, *not least.*] H. Perforans:—The
Bore; L'Embêtant. *Vultu imperturbabili; patientiâ inex-
haustâ; linguâ immensurabili; auribus nullis, aut pror-
sùs obturatis. Passim, Hierichunte exceptâ.* H. nodiceps:
—La papillottèe. *Matutina; crinibus papyro implicitis;
cætera "simplex munditiis."* (*Nurseries and breakfast
rooms.*) H. nephelegeretes:—The Cloud-blower. (*Habitat,*

the leaves of Nicotiana tabacum, rarely visible.) See Virgil,
Æn. i. 411, &c. H. Gypæetus:—The Gyp. *Facundus,
alacris, acer; pedibus-velox, manibus velocior, linguâ ve-
locissimus. (Habitat, Cambridge, in and about the Col-
leges; type, Old Rose.)* H. Lectisterna:—The Bedmaker.
*Lenta, secura; linguâ volubili, manibus ambidextris.
(Ibid; type, Mrs. Hopper.)* H. auriga:—Der Kutscher;
Il vetturino; the Coachie of old authors; Naso respectabili,
rubro; cubitis quadratis; humeris rotundatis (est qui "mutat
quadrata rotundis,") pilei margine latissimo parùm recurvo;
voce nunc sibilante, mox raucissimâ; oculo sesqui-altero
subinde semi-apertiusculo; (non raro lippescente) exuviis
crassissimis albis; bullis (" buttons ") diobolum æquantibus,
margaritomaternis; type, Brummagem Bill, nearly extinct:
confined to unfrequented districts. (Vide Tabulas Georgii
Scolioscelis apud Fastos Comicos.) H. aurigaster:—The
Cabbie (late Jarvy). Priore duplo minor; pileo Jacobo-
crovio vel Vidavaco; nonnunquam umbonato; Supertoto
caoutchato glaberrimo; digito indice sæpissimè sublato.
Fully described and figured by Charivarius and Leech, in
their great 4to work, De rummis unis, cum hominibus tum
veheterinis ac jumentis. Veneunt apud Tiltum et Bogum
Viâ Classiariâ Londoni.

In following up this subject, it is encouraging to find
the groups so strictly natural that, instead of having to seek
for them, they force themselves upon our notice in every
walk (and in every "walk of *life*"). Any one who has
access to the voluminous work of Charivarius (Vol. xlvi. just
out !) might multiply very tranchant varieties, " as thick as
mill-wheels strike." *We* have been particularly struck of
late with instances in which male and female types are so
patent-ly correlative that they might without impropriety
be called, in Baconian phrase, Instantiæ *se-registrantes*. We
subjoin a few of these parallels:—

ADAMIDÆ.   EVIDÆ.

" Ubi tu Caius, ibi ego Caia."

a H. curtinolecturatus. Prostratus, imbellis ; pilio exili, conico, fastigiato: oculis conniventibus ; voce suffocatiusculâ. Habitat ubique in oppidis, ruri rarior, (type, Mr. Caudle ; vide Charivar. et Leech de rummis unis, &c.)

β H. volens. synonyms, H. felix mas, Der Selbstherrscher.

γ H. heelsupwardius. synon., H. spiflicatus, Le boulversé. passim apud Anglos.

a H. curtinolecturans. erecta, bellicosissima ; pileo patulo, limbifero, gofferato, oculis bipatentibus ; voce " tubæ æmulâ," ad finem raucescente. Habitat ibid ; type, Mrs. C. apud eosdem.

β H. nolens-volens. synon. H. infelix fæmina, Impotentilla anserina.

γ H. upsettivola. synon., H. spiflicans, H. fortis animi, La boulversante. Ibid.

Note.—Since those days (1864), *H. fortis animi was seen and heard at Norwich ; and H. giftus gabbi, perched on stumps, in several counties, last Autumn.*

REVIEW: JULIUS CÆSAR,

AN author of some note, in certain circles, on account of his "immortal Commentaries" and his mortal aversion to good-for-nothing officers. Least known where he is most wanted ; for, though an eminent commander, he fails to command the attention of Her Majesty's forces ; and I am credibly informed that, in the apartment somewhat rudely termed the " *mess*-room," the Gallic War has given place to Tupper's Proverbial Philosophy. When forced to swim for his life, our author is said to have seized the MS. in his teeth, in usum studiosæ juventutis, worse luck for *them ;* and in fact some *biting* sarcasms are still met with in the printed editions. See Book I., chap. 40. For want of a better (*i.e.* of a *military*) edition, try George Long's, and read his preface and introduction.

N.B.—The poem beginning, " Arma virum que cano,"

which an army man might naturally ascribe to the warlike author of the Commentaries, is, with far more probability, fathered upon a practical farmer, called Virgil, whose Mother, if not a mantua-maker by trade, yet, as she certainly lived at Mantua, where she gave birth to the poet, ["Mantua me genuit,"] *was*, in that sense, the *making of Mantua*, otherwise an obscure little place.

REVIEW: BIBLE (HOLY).

A New Translation, according to the Letter and Idioms of the Original Languages, (21s. 6d.,) by Robert Young, Esq.

HAVING had a specimen of this work presented to us by a worthy clergyman, whose heart's desire seems to be the diffusion of God's truth, we have read carefully the Epistle to the Galatians, and looked into some others. Referring our readers to remarks in the Introduction to *Adversaria, (i.e., short notes,) on the Greek Testament, (No. I. p. 35,) we never saw, nor expected to see, those remarks so thoroughly illustrated in any *serious* book. The few samples given in p. 36, on purpose to exhibit the futility of "literal rendering," are not a whit more unmeaning than many and many a passage in Mr. Young's so-called Translation. For instance, "declared righteous by works of law shall be no flesh;" "your eyes having plucked out, ye would have given to me;" "against such law is not." It is impossible to learn a second language (suppose French) properly, without discovering that it presents two striking features; the new *words* and the new *idioms:* so that plenty of sen-

* We were well punished for this *richly pedantic* title, on finding that a worthy friend concluded, from the resemblance to "Adversaries," that the articles must be eminently pugilistic! *Don't* we pay for aping Porson?

tences might be so translated, or rather mangled, that, though containing nothing but English *words*, yet they would not be the English *language* at all. Thus, "How you carry you?" "I not see than you;" "It there has of the men," are not English expressions, either good or bad, though not containing a single French word—Mr. Young appears to ignore this feature of *language in general.* He has great abundance of such non-English in his "New Translation." Besides this, he also ignores the Greek language in particular; rendering, for instance, Gal. i. 4, " God, even our Father," instead of " our God and Father;" ver. 7, "except there *be*," instead of " only there *are ;*" chap. ii. 6, "whatever they were *once*," for "whatever they were ;" iii. 21, " if *the* law was given which was able ;" for "if there had been *a* law given which was able ;" v. 12, " O that—and they shall cut themselves off," for "I would they were even cut off;" 17, "that the things which ye may *not* will—these ye may do," for " so that ye should *not do* the things that ye *would.*" Another language which he ignores is English: *e.g.*, "the good *news* that *were* proclaimed by me, that *it is* not according to man ;" " dissemb*led* with him *did* the other Jews." The banishment of the familiar words *church*, angel, *tradition*, gospel, *Gentiles*, everlasting—for which are substituted *assembly*, messenger, *deliverance*, good news, *nations*, age-during—even supposing them *all* improvements in the abstract, would render the New Translation a book very puzzling to *the people*, till they should be educated on purpose to understand them. On the back of this specimen are advertised seventeen "Biblical" works by Mr. Young, of the collective value of £6 12s. We hope they are not all executed in the same manner. The impression left on our own mind is that there is no more charm in being an Esquire

than a Reverend, since we find such *very* slender clerks
in each class. If this last deserves to be called a "critical
opinion," we beg that our name, "Old Price," be added
to the 45 (qu. "the auld 45?" at least half of them are
Scots) who figure at the foot, or perhaps *at the feet,* of the
seventeen works, as "Members of TEN different denomi-
nations"! We will only add that if some really good
Grecian north of Tweed would, instead of solecistic English, give us a Testament in his own noble language, (not
dialect, says Latham,) without affecting English idioms at
all, we should treat such a translation with great respect.

ON THE PUN; WITH A PUN OR TWO WRITTEN:
BY A PUN-DIT.

GOOD Puns, and especially of the class called "good bad
puns," form an excellent gymnastic exercise in the study of
Words and of Language. It may stand very low in the scale
of wit and humour—be it so; it has its educational value,
in sharpening the faculties for higher attainments. For
this reason I consider puns far too serious for LEVIORA, and
place them under the head of Philology. Were I to say
that a certain country in Europe was the very opposite to a
bankruptcy in the city, it might not immediately occur to
the G. R. that I meant Westphalia; and yet, on reflection,
East is not *more* opposed to West than East failure to West
failure! A *Riddle* presented in this form sets the mind a
sifting and comparing words and thoughts with a degree of
diligence which it would be difficult to induce by any mere
matter-of-fact questioning. The pun may be an atrocious
one—a vile perpetration—an insult to *both* the E. and W.
end, and to every Postal district of our enlightened metro-

polis. We wont stop to defend *it ;* but the question is, can it set young brains to work, with the hopeful request : "Don't *tell* me." Then I rejoice over it, more than over any mere "piece of wit." By the bye, when We were in London in 1856, Victoria Street, Westminster, appeared to be a kind of West failure. There was a noble row of houses laid out in a novel style—most, if not all, being "Flats," a great many of which were untenanted. Our hostess had most comfortable apartments, though We think there were 80 steps to get up to them ; but then the Land-lord had considerately established most comfortable stuffed settees on the landings for his tenants and their visitors *(and laundresses !)* to "Rest and be thankful." That this was not the highest flat either, We can positively testify, for We went *up stairs* to get a better view of that grand but grievous sight, the conflagration at Broadwood's Piano Manufactory ! But it was said to be exactly on the level of Woburn Square, and therefore enjoyed a very superior stratum of atmosphere to that of the average environs.

Hence, in this favoured locality, those who pass the day in sedentary employments, may find a house where their greatest desiderata, "air and exercise," are to be attained not only to an amount $=$ the Square *in* the distance, but varying inversely as the Rent, which is naturally obliged to sink in order to oblige those who are obliged to rise, **vi et cruribus*, above their humble neighbours, *telling stories,* 1, 2, 3, or more, all the way up to their own door ! Now, what is more rich and rare—τί σπανιωτερον;—than to pay less for what *you* value most ? And We well remember, in those days, feeling the great advantage of our station, as "aeriæ palumbes," *(when once we got there)* with the charming

---

* An obvious Hendiadys for a strong pair of legs. "Cf pateris et auro." Virg.

bird's-eye view of that old deserted garden of Plane trees, Hawthorns, &c., run wild, and swarming with old and young members of that merry society of free and easy gamins, the House Sparrows. These, persecuted in the barbarous Country, find a crumb and welcome, every where in Town, where they barely get out of the way of carriages, horses, and pedestrians ; and, in the Royal Botanic Gardens, boldly enter the Refreshment room and hop about the floor, claiming a share with characteristic bonhommie, not to say bondiablerie. But they must not fly away with *us*, G. R., as they do with the crusts. So—one word more in favour of our dear old quarters, where We were not surprised in 1862 to find fewer houses " VOID," as they have it at Bath. Suppose it be urged that *rheumatism* is a decided objection to an elevation requiring rampant habits and a warranty of " sound wind and *limb*." We shall simply reply by an Enigma of the class above prescribed as a mental exercise, and here as a bodily medicine into the bargain, viz.: What . is the best homœopathic residence for neuralgic subjects?

———

IN quoting ὥσπερ τους ἐχεῖς, I formerly indulged my Learned Readers with a circumflex, *non* "sicut meus est mos." I wonder how many were any wiser for that pretty looking accent with which I used to thatch a syllable here and there at school, just as I thought most conducive to ornamentation. I remember a band of tolerable scholars (Butlerian preposters, G. R.,) being floored by that very expression, notwithstanding the little crooked mark ! It was pretty generally translated, " those whom thou hast." And *I know who*, with kind intention no doubt, dropped in, under false pretences, to the " Dancing school," where

I had stayed hammering my brains at it to the last, and slipped a paper into my hand with the word "Vipers." I would *not* say, dear old schoolfellow (J. S. S.), that " Hell is paved with good intentions" of *that* class, and I have a word to say, one of these days, respecting that awful adage: but I *would* warn School Boys and Girls, that there is no *real* kindness in assisting each other in deception of *any* kind. "Dulce est *desipere* in loco ;" do not say *decipere*.

THE ANCIENTS SURPASSED.

AMONG the proofs of fidelity in slaves, we find, in a well known passage, " Porrigere cervicem pro domino," "stretching out their neck for the master," mentioned as the *ne plus ultra* of devotion. How servants must have improved in the interim! It is quite a common thing, now-a-days, for one *or more* to be ready to do this on the most trifling occasions, and with the shortest notice, *to see if Master's coming,* and give notice to the rest.

THE CHILD IS FATHER TO THE MAN.

" ὁ παις πατηρ μεν ἐστι τ'ανδρος·" ἐυ λεγεις·
πατηρ δ'ἐγω του παιδος· ἀλλ' ἀνηρ ὁ παις·
ἐλαθον ἐμαυτον παππος ὡν; κομιδη μεν ὀυν.

LE METTE CURCE MALGRÈ LUI.
Duoglot Elegiaes.

Attonitus stuck fast medio Topsawerus actu,
Where on earth, mirans, alter old fellow foret:
On earth! Coalmini laquear getting thinner and thinner,
At last, audires "crack," and away the chap went!

"Ut ex tam *alto* dignitatis gradu ad *inferos* videatur deos potiùs quam ad *superos* pervenisse." To be sure Lælius, speaking of Scipio Africanus minor, says (De Amic. 3), "ad *superos* potius quam ad *inferos;*" but then Scipio was a *Top*-sawyer. Not so our Mettus Curtius, whose great predecessor leapt into the gulf, because, as I was lately informed at Shrewsbury, he considered it "a fine opening for a young man."

OLD SAWS SHARPENED, &c.

Edged tools, in great variety, at Old Prices.

"πολλα μοι ὑπ' ἀγκωνος ὠκεα βελη."—*Pindar.*

Lucus à non lucendo: rectè Domine; *Quidni igitur* Vacatio, à non vacando?

One of O. P.'s best pupils was an Echo at the passage of the Great Culvert between Birkenhead and Poolton. Observing that she was, "previous to lessons from Mr. P.," able to repeat seven English syllables very distinctly, he took her in hand; and, in an incredibly short time, "*after* d°. d°., from Mr. D°.," she would reply in *French, German,* &c., to questions asked in the vernacular. For instance, if a School-boy consulted this Pythia thus, "Sam has a holiday to-day—may *we?*" She would answer, most good-naturedly, "Mais oui!" and so on. G. R. wilt thou *carry out* this linguistic suggestion?

PROBLEM.

Think a page of French *without words,* and then translate it into German thoughts, *d°. d°.*

THE PHENOMENON OF THE DAY.—*Mar.* 10, 1863.

THE ARRIVAL OF THE PRINCESS OF WALES.

I. Εἴδωλον Ὁμήρου προλογιζει (βουκολικωτερον, ἀτε τοῖς τοιουτοις ἐν Αἴδου ὁμιλησας).

Τίς ποθεν ἀδ᾽ ἀ ᾽νθρωπος ; " Α᾽λεξανδρΑ θεοειδης ! "
Τις ποτ᾽ Α᾽λεξανδρΑ; τον Παριν ὀιδα μονον.

II. O. P., as a *Dee sided, if not a decided, naturalist, congratulates H.R.H. the Prince of Wales, on having imported to the favoured shores of his Island Home,

Geologically, the most interesting of all recent littoral deposits.

Mineralogically, "a Gem of purest ray serene."

Botanically, a choice specimen of the FLORA DANICA.

Zoologically, a bright Beröid of the Baltic.

Anthropologically, a PRINCESS, a LADY, and (best of all) a WOMAN—for,

" Ein Weib ist das ehrlichste Ding."—*Old song in Mozart's Works.*

THE PHENOMENON OF THE DAY,

JAN. 8, 1868.—*Scene, Frogmore.*

Quibus, Hector, ab oris,
Expectate (?) venis?—*Virgil.*

Α᾽ρχουσα ποντου κλυθι μοῦ Βρεταννια!
Τίς, οὐσα πεντηκοντα δη μειων ἐτων,
Δισσους ἀνασσα δητ ἀνακτας ἐβλεπεν,
Αὐτη γ᾽ ἑαυτης; τουθ᾽ ὀρα Γικτωρια,
Τῃδ᾽ ἡμερᾳ, τεκνον τε καὶ τεκνου τεκνον!

A LOCUS CLASSICUS IN 1863.

At the Odeum, Queer Street.

ONE of the most charming sights in London, always except-

---

* " Dee-sided," *i.e.*, presented by the late Prince Consort with a copy of Dee-side.

ing a certain royal carriage in Hyde Park, is our friend, O. D., gracefully reposing—yes, repose is the very word— on our own sofa, waving his lily hand to the myrmidons who fly at his bidding, and issuing his few but peremptory orders with the calm *self*-possession (and what could he possess more precious?) of a man who is par negotiis *atque* suprà, and with the easy unaffected condescension of one who *knows* rather than *feels* his position as joint-proprietor of a large and important establishment, and who needs not to labour, as some do, to *make* those around him know who's who. The refinement of his early education throws an Augustan grace over the most ordinary transactions and phrases of the trade, and renders Queer Street Bazaar no less an Academia of elegantiæ than an emporium of utilities. As the "stout boy," now restored to average dimensions, passes that resting place (the very centre and type of otium cum dignitate,) O. D. will point to the shutter—and, with an arch smile, tell him to come into the shop next morning either *with* it or *on* it. " Persicos odi, puer, apparatus," means " away with that sample of *Persian!*" " Favete linguis," " girls! don't chatter so incessantly;" and he sometimes soliloquizes, " Non sum qualis eram," but in no repining tone. His photogram, taken in 1853, is a killing bait to country customers; (we wish O. P.'s may be half as effective in town—" plures adnabunt thynni et cetaria crescent,") and, though *he* considers himself villainously fallen away in the intervening decad, *we* might still say very handsome things of him. But query, who is O.D.?—*Nous Verrons.*

COINAGE.

" WHAT do I mean by Metosmose?" What? Why, the old " Endosmose *and* Exosmose " in one expressive word; better than respiration names a function including the two acts of *in-*spiration and *expiration*. The word was wanted, and I made it; perhaps 25 years ago; and if my ungrateful country wont have it, even so was a Cæsar treated. *Other* words are wanted : I shall try again. Ego invideor ? asks Horace, coining *that very word* at the same moment!

AMONGST the many fallacies by which youthful minds are victimized in our day, I lately heard the following :—That, all language being confessedly imperfect, truth, *for which we have no vehicle but language*, is manifestly unattainable: everything *professing* to be truth *must* be impaired by the defective medium through which it is conveyed; so that an absolute verity is impossible. The answer is simply this: Language, though defective, is *very far* from being defective *to that extent*. *Ambiguous* terms form a *part*, not the *whole*, of any given language; and it would be almost idle to give examples of a thing so common as statements which are *perfectly* true, and so devoid of any ambiguity whatever as to be *incapable of two meanings*.

TO A KIND OLD FRIEND, (BISHOP GRAHAM,) WITH A PRESENT
OF " OLD PRICE'S REMAINS."

Accept, indulgent friend, this book,
To take with you from home:
Nor room nor weight of this is great,
Wherever you may roam.
Since other *ANA* have been all the go,
Try Price's *ΛΕΙΨ-ANA* ; and what for no?

On a little mystic book, entitled " Selecta é Præscriptis."

Selecta è *Præscriptis?* Pshaw! dissimulation vain is:
We twig at once our old school friend, "Selectæ è *Profanis*."

PHOTO*gram* stands or falls with tele*gram*. I studied the controversy at the time, and kept the letters in the *Times*. Of course Shilleto was right; I say " of course," because Shilleto is an old Shrewsbury man, or Butlerian R.S.S.A., and also a Trinity man, a Porson Prize man, &c., &c.; besides which, he is Dick Shilleto: and who *should* be right in a purely *Greek* question if Dick is wrong? But, in an *English* question, John Bull is supreme; and he *will* have Tele*gram* to match (as he thinks) diagram and anagram. And, if the shade of Dick Porsons's self " came again" to insist on Telegrapheme, John would only laugh at him, and say, " Larn yer Granny."

OLD SAWS SHARPENED, &c. .

Edged tools, in great variety, at Old Prices.
"πολλα μοι ὑπ' ἀγκωνος ὠκεα βελη."—*Pindar.*

AB (*you* know) disce omnes; since it is always best to proceed from the *known* to the *unknown*.

"In cute curandâ plus *equo* operata juventus ;" repugnante metro, sensu tamen optimo; scil. in currying their hide; more than (many) a horse gets.

"Tanto conspectius in se Crimen habet, quanto major qui peccat habetur" *Juv.* Hence : The greater the *saint*, the greater the *sinner.*

Artis est celare artem. It is the province of Art to conceal art. Few precepts are more strictly attended to. Go to any exhibition of pictures, and you shall see good store of performances, where the concealment is so perfect, that *not the smallest trace* of Art is discoverable by the unassisted eye.

Of what vehicle does Cæsar repeatedly speak ? Of " his *omnibus.*" Bell. Gall. " Subsequebatur *omnibus*," lib. 2, cap. 19; " *ex* omnibus," cap. 29; " *cum* omnibus," 4, 21 ; " *in* omnibus," 4, 23 ; "omnibus," passim. Did it run without opposition ? Not quite. " His omnibus *unum repugnabat*"

AN IMPORTANT OMISSION.
"It is not painful, my Pætus."—*Rom. Hist.*

A modern Arria, quite a model wife,
Tired of her spouse, but not quite tired of life,
Doing the tragic cheap, forgetful elf,
Hands him the sword ; *omits to stab herself.*

WHOSE Missis was " Missis Ambagibus ?" and where did she live ? The Ambages were once placed, off hand, " in Asia Minor." (At T. C. D.)

ONE may " perform an elephant " by impersonating him, inside a pachyderm hide of pasteboard ; or else (Hiphil) by *making him,* (*i.e.,* a *performing* elephant,) go through certain evolutions.

ADVERSARIA ON THE GREEK TESTAMENT.

MUCH misapprehension prevails, both amongst the learned and unlearned, as to the advantages possessed in regard to a thorough understanding of the New Testament by *ordinary* Greek scholars. These last look down upon the mere English reader, and the other looks up to them, with pity and envy, " each to each." Both are labouring under a delusion which I should be glad to dissipate at the outset of these comments. On the one hand, the unlettered Englishman, if he be of that pains-taking class which Bishop Horsley truly honours with the name of " learned Christians," (see his excellent preface,) has no reason to envy the superiority derived from the little Greek that is usually known by average classical scholars ; on the other hand, the οἱ πολλοι in classics are under a very serious mistake if they feel entitled to pronounce on any delicate questions respecting the original text of the New Testament. I believe I am (1850) acquainted with *one* man who is qualified to speak authoritatively on this very important and interesting subject. He has paid attention not only to Attic Greek, with the dialects as given in school grammars, but to Byzantine and Alexandrian writers, so as to appreciate the tendencies and gradual transition to modern Greek, with which he is also familiar. For a man who has none of this *kind* of acquaintance with the language to set up as a competent textuary is neither wise nor fair; whilst the *minimum* (which too often proves the *maximum*) at examinations for Orders furnishes perhaps the most striking illustration of the adage, "A little knowledge is a dangerous thing."

There is also a delusion prevalent regarding the value of a "literal rendering" of the Scriptures. Where the idiom of the original happens to agree exactly with our own, of course literalism not only is desirable but becomes, practically, a matter of course; and the unlearned reader may be assured that in such passages the translators did not in general *go out of their way* to give us any other than this easiest and most obvious imitation of the original. But, when the idioms do *not* agree, then a literal rendering is of no use to the unlearned, and can only serve the philological purpose of assisting the student to apprehend the peculiarity of the dead language; for as to the *meaning*, a translation of such a phrase, "verbatim," often gives no meaning at all in English, but makes mere nonsense, especially if the *order* of the words be also preserved as in the original. We need not go far in search of instances of this.—*e.g.* in Rom. i. 7, we should have, "To all the being in Rome;" in verse 15, "Thus the according to me foreminded;" in Rom. ii. 28, preserving the *order*, we should have, "Not for the in the manifest Jew is;" in iii. 29, again, "Or of Jews the God alone ? not but and of Gentiles ?" and so forth. (See page 73.)

Now surely, in these instances, we have to thank the translators for preferring the exact *meaning* of the Greek to a version which, though verbally (=literally, and a better word)—though verbally correct, would fail to convey any meaning at all, or else mislead by a wrong one. It is just the blue ink of page 13 which has a *right* to ignore meaning.

So far am I from an *over*-weening estimate of the knowledge of Greek for the sake of the New Testament, that I have dissuaded several adult friends from taking up the study with that view. My own persuasion is that, unless in the providence of God, that privilege has been enjoyed in early life, (in which case it should be used thankfully,) our own excellent version may well content them under some confessed disadvantages respecting a few, *very* few, mistranslated passages, and a larger number of others, where, from the very nature of the Babel diversity, a *brighter* idea of the meaning is attained, than any other language besides the original could be expected to convey. And, the appreciation of this higher luminosity of that which is already highly luminous, would hardly be attained by ὀψιμαθεις (late learners).

N.B.—However early *you* begin, my *young* friends, I have stronger grounds for recommending the study of Greek (with or without Latin) to all the highly educated youths of both sexes, than any real *spiritual* advantage it could give you over earnest searchers of the English or Welsh New Testament. And, I think, I might say the same of the French and German. Beyond these languages, I should be speaking at random ; though I did, formerly, venture to " deffer wid " his Lordship of Segovia, (p. 91) as to his *Spanish* rendering of Rom. i. 3, 4. *(See Introduction.)*

ETERNITY IS TIME'S SUPERLATIVE.

A "Night Thought" omitted by Young —— supplied by Old ——
and recommended to Young and Old.

THE thought occurred to me in connection with the expression αιων αιωνων for Eternity, which may perhaps be considered as a kind of superlative of αιων, as Rex regum of Rex.

It is worth while to consider the various equivalents of this expression. "For ever," "for evermore," "for ever and ever," are the renderings, and I believe true renderings, of nine different expressions in the Greek Testament, viz.: (1)—εἰς τον αιωνα; (2)—εἰς τους αιωνας; (3)—εἰς τους αιωνας των αιωνων; (4)—εἰς τον αιωνα του αιωνος, Heb. i. 8; (5)—εἰς αιωνα; 2 Peter, ii. 17; (6)—εἰς ἡμεραν αιωνος, 2 Peter, iii. 18; (7)—εἰς παντας τους αιωνας, Jude 25; (8)—εἰς αιωνας αιωνων, Rev. xiv. 11; and, (9)—εἰς πασας τας γενεας του αιωνος των αιωνων, Eph. iii. 21. The three first, marked 1, 2, 3, (as in that useful book, the Englishman's Greek Concordance,) are of very frequent occurence; of the six others, each occurs but once, viz., in the texts specified; whilst αιων αιωνων, though *intended* by the writer for a quotation, does not occur at all! Now it is difficult to say which is the most sublime of these groups of *very* few words, chosen by the Holy Spirit to express an idea which is in itself one of transcendent sublimity. Can anything surpass in grandeur the first of these, εἰς τον αιωνα, " for *the* age?" conveying the great truth that Eternity is, essentially, one unbroken stream of time. But again, the second, εἰς τους αιωνας, expresses, as briefly as possible, the other fact, that Eternity is one infinite whole which includes many finite periods. And if these two are glorious and magnificent, what shall we say to the third, which is both plural and (in the sense proposed at the outset) superlative? viz., εἰς τοὺς αἰῶνας τῶν αἰώνων—"to the ages of the ages," which the anarthrous Latin more feebly renders by " In sæcula sæculorum." The fourth is interesting as the exact counterpart of the third, only in the singular number; the fifth is a repetition of the first, only without the article. The sixth, "to a day of an age," or, "the day of the age" (?) (anarthrous, however—no article with *either* noun), reminds us of the two grand converses: " with the Lord a thousand years are as one day, and one day as a thousand years ;" and it is well indeed to be reminded of this, amidst the difficulties which beset, apparently by Divine appointment (Acts i. 7), the study of prophetic chronology. The seventh merely fills up the virtual ellipsis of πάντας, which occurs in the second. The eighth, on the contrary, is an anarthrous repetition of the third. [*No contrast is, I believe, conveyed by the absence of the article in any of these cases (?)*] The ninth is the longest, and the most remarkable of all—a pregnant paragraph of itself, carrying the mind through a longer flight, " φροντίδος πλανοις," than, perhaps, any other eight words ever written or uttered, either by man or God—" Unto all the generations of the age of the ages." Even in English, the words, as well as the conception, roll on with majestic solemnity; but in the Greek, eminently " ore rotundo." This phrase occurs in Eph. iii. 21, and is here placed after the rest, as a grand finale, in virtue of its surpassing weight and dignity. It not only suggests, by " τοῦ αἰῶνος," the vast illimitable unit—the unbroken vista, without even an *apparent* vanishing point, down which the yearning eye of a mind at peace with God (and if not, *why not?* see John i. 12) rejoices, yet with trembling, to gaze wistfully at times ; but, also, by " τῶν αἰώνων," it presents before us the multitudinous plurality—the " innumerabilis

annorum series, et fuga temporum"—the long succession of
centuries, chiliads, and dispensations, of which our little
sample, called time, is circumstantially made up.* But,
moreover, the human interest in those revolving eras, is
awakened by " τας γενεας," the generations that are to enter
and quit the stage of life during the totality of those un-
told cycles. And, still further to enhance this last idea, we
have " πασας"—all, to the very last generation on earth—
the " quick," whom Jesus will come to judge in the great
and terrible day of the Lord.

Had Longinus taken this passage in hand instead of
Genesis i., he might well have introduced it with Παυλος
ουχ ὁ τυχων ἀνηρ! But, a greater than Paul is here.

The adjective derived from ἀιων, and, I should say, em-
bodying all these modifications of it, is ἀιωνιος: yet a much
esteemed and lamented friend, in the pursuit of a favourite
doctrine, either invented himself, or accepted as a valuable
invention, the English adjective " æonian " as its equivalent;
on the ground that " eternal" and " everlasting," by which
αἰωνιος is represented in the authorised version, do *not* convey its true meaning. I confess this always seemed to me
an admission that the Greek word conveyed to *his* mind no
idea whatever; since to call it "æonian" is, in fact, to leave
it *un*translated, like Selah in the Psalms.

ROMANS, i. 1—7.

I ONCE made for my own use, (many, many years ago,) a
translation of this most remarkable passage; because the
authorised version seemed so much less clearly to express
the great truths conveyed in it than the Original Greek, in

* Think'st thou existence doth depend on time?
It doth ; but *actions are our epochs.*—MANFRED.
12

which there is not the slightest obscurity. This inferiority arises, not from any errors on the part of the translators, but from a less capacity in the English language for parenthetic arrangement; so that it would hardly be possible to do justice to so long a sentence without breaking it up into two or three: a procedure which, in a few other instances also, would perhaps have relieved the English Testament from periods "involved" to an extent unsuited to the genius of the language. I can not at present lay my hand upon the above *ancient* rendering of my own: but, on referring to a fine copy of the original [Cantabrigiæ, apud Thos. Buck. Anno Domini 1632. Copperplate title page, with a stag drinking at a pump-cistern.] I find the punctuation exactly what I proposed, viz: with the second verse in one parenthesis, and the third, from " which was made," down to the end of the fourth, included in another; the words *Ιησου Χριστου του Κυριου ημων* then follow, out of parenthesis, whilst a third parenthesis includes the fifth and sixth verses. If my reader will draw these six brackets with a pencil, the perspicuity of that notation will, I believe, be so apparent that he will not be disposed to rub them out. Our translators, feeling the infirmity of their language in the above particular, have brought up the words "Jesus Christ our Lord" from the end of the fourth verse, which is their true Greek position, to the middle of the third, which (for the said reason) is more natural for English. In examining other translations, I see that the difficulty has been generally felt as to modern languages; some taking the same liberty as ourselves with these four words, others leaving them at their Greek distance from "his Son," but strengthening the weak point by " c'est à dire," " nemlich," " te weten," " namliga," "convem a saber," &c., (all="to wit.")

In the Dutch and Portuguese (as well as Beza's Latin)

the three parentheses are marked exactly as in my old
Greek Testament; whilst the Bishop of Segovia, not seeing
the parenthetic character of the passage at all, has both
misplaced and mistranslated the four words egregiously ;
giving " por la resurrection de Jesu Christo Senor nuestro,"
instead of the *very* clear rendering in the Catalan (query by
an *Arch*bishop ?)—" per *sa* resurrecio," which gives *the only
possible sense,* since that "resurrection from the dead" by
which Jesus was declared to be the Son of God with power,
could be no other than *his own* personal resurrection on the
predicted 3rd day, whereas the Spanish makes " his Son,"
verse 3, appear to be *a different person* from " Jesus Christ
our Lord" in the fourth verse! To proceed, however, with
the English. I attach great importance to the right understanding of this passage, because I believe the divinity of
Jesus to be at least as essential to the work of saving his
people from their sins as his humanity, [Jehovah has said
"Beside ME there is no Saviour,"] and because I think that
doctrine is revealed here in strong and plain terms. If
κατα σαρκα be understood to mean *on the mother's side,* and
κατα πνευμα *on the father's side,* then the whole sentence
seems consistent and clear. But, if κατα σαρκα be taken to
include Joseph as well as Mary, κατα πνευμα is left to seek
a place which cannot be found for it anywhere : in the 1st
place, because, as a mere fact, there *is* no " tertium-quid;"
and, in the next place, how or in what sense could the
resurrection declare *a mere man* " to be the Son of God with
power, according to the Spirit of Holiness ?" I strongly
suspect that to believe one *can* extract sense—any what-
soever—from the sentence thus interpreted, is (as Bryce says
in the invaluable " Note B" to his Algebra) to " deliver our
understandings into captivity to a jargon of unmeaning
words." On the other hand, Jesus had claimed to be the

Son of God, and one with the Father, in such a way that the unbelieving Jews, who called him " the carpenter's son," understood him to assume equality with God, and accused him roundly of blasphemy. But it was no more blasphemy than the still more explicit annunciation to the Virgin: " The Holy Ghost shall come upon thee, and the power of the highest shall overshadow thee ; therefore, also that holy thing which shall be born of thee shall be called the Son of God ;" a passage which is in exact accordance with our text here, and was the answer vouchsafed to that blessed woman who *asked no further question*, but " kept *all* these things, and pondered them in her heart!" (Luke ii. 19.) and again (verse 51.) " Kept *all* these sayings in her heart." They were *worth* keeping : and may God help *us*, who have the very same need of them that she had, to ponder them in the same humble spirit of *subdued enquiry*. (Compare verse 34. with 38.)

In looking once more at the original, I confess I hardly hope to convey to the mere English reader *my own conviction* of the clearness with which these clauses, in their native *position* as Greek, and by the plain *meaning* of each individual word, convey the doctrine of a twofold nature ; one derived from his human royal mother, the other from no human father, but from God exclusively. After naming " his Son," the apostle, under the dictation of the Holy Ghost, inserts a parenthesis, explaining *in what sense* he was the Son of God, viz: that, whilst on the *human* side, he was a descendant of David, on the *divine* side he was declared, by his resurrection from the dead, to be God's Son in power. The resurrection, let me here observe, is the *cardinal* point of the truth of Christianity : upon it everything may be said to " hinge." The enemies said that, if *that* should be received as a fact, their party would receive the most deadly blow; as they very intelligibly expressed it, "the last error shall be worse than the first." If "that deceiver," who *said* "after three days I will rise again," should be believed to have actually *done* so, it would be vain to call him any more "a deceiver." Hence the importance to *them* of *falsifying* the resurrection. Matt. xxviii. 12—15. Now, when *the Lord was risen indeed*, he had, by that one fact, confirmed the truth of that and of *every other* assertion and claim he had ever made in his life; of which, assuredly, by *far* the strongest, the most critical, and decisive was his claim to Sonship, in such terms as John v. 23; and to oneness with the Father, as in John x. 30; and to priority to Abraham, as in John viii. 58; and to the world itself, as in John xviii. 5. All of which, if not substantiated, were so plainly blasphemous that the unbelievers treated him as a blasphemer without ceremony on several occasions. But this crowning miracle *did* substantiate everything, to the comfort of his blindly despairing followers. Hence the importance to *them* of *verifying* the resurrection: for this great purpose the traitor's place was filled up by a true man—Matthias, Acts i. 22. This was the grand subject of testimony: "This Jesus hath God raised up *whereof we are all witnesses.*" Acts ii. 32. See also, in the "Evangelical sermons" of that day, how important a place this doctrine *then* held. Acts ii. 24—32; iii. 15; iv. 10 and 33; v. 31; x. 40; xiii. 30—37; xviii. 3 and 18; xxvi. 23. It is, then, not difficult to understand how Jesus Christ, after being put to death as an impostor—as one who, being a man, made himself God,— was most clearly defined, or definitely marked out, (ὁρισθεντος) as the Son of God in power, by his resurrection from the dead.

As to individual words—First: ὁρίζω (from ὁρος a limit), occurs eight times in the New Testament, and is translated everywhere else either "determine," "ordain," or "limit." It gives the English their word "Horizon," the limiting circle of our view. Its compound, ἀφωρισμενος just above in verse 1, is "separated."

If one were to hunt the Lexicons for a verb better calculated to express not merely declaration but demarcation, by a tranchant line, from everything else with which he might be confounded, I do not think we could satisfy ourselves better with any other than ὁρίζω; not even χωρίζω (Heb. vii. 26), which is the verb chosen by the Spirit to denote his separation from sinners. He *might* have been, "as was supposed, the son of Joseph" (Luke iii. 23); he *was* absolutely marked out, by his resurrection, to be what he had plainly declared himself to be—the Son of God in power, one with his Father, and whom his prophet had long before announced as "Wonderful, Counsellor, the Mighty God, the Everlasting Father, the Prince of Peace" (Isa. ix. 6.)

2. δυναμις. This noun has an extended signification, from the very highest to the very lowest sense of the English word, "power." It would be absurd to seek parallels to this passage amongst the lower acceptations of δυναμις, which occurs about 120 times in the New Testament. The passage already quoted from Luke i. 35, has it, with reference to the conception of Jesus, and gives this very reason why he should be called *God's Son*, ὑιος θεου (as here, *without articles*). In Mat. xxvi. 64, he predicts his own second advent, and describes himself "sitting on the right hand of *power*." In 1 Cor. i. 24, he is himself called "the *power* of God, and the wisdom of God."

. In contending, therefore, for the very highest expression of personal divinity in these words, "the Son of God with power," I am not conscious of straining terms (as one may easily do) to support a favourite doctrine ; for a favourite doctrine it may well be, with those who believe the son of *Joseph* and Mary, could no more save them than they could save themselves.

3. κατα σαρκα—κατα πνευμα, are so placed, in their respective clauses, as essentially and indisputably to point to *some two* things : and if these two be not equivalent to " *the mother's side* " and "*the father's side*," as we commonly speak of relationships, I am utterly at a loss for any possible meaning to be assigned the words, " according to the spirit of holiness." I am surprised not to find them, in any version, translated " the Holy Spirit," after the analogy of Col. i. 13, where " Son of his love " is rendered " dear Son."   I have but one remark more to offer, viz., on the absence of the articles with ἀναστασεως νεκρων.   I believe them to be omitted because *the context seems sufficiently* to show that it *must* be ἡ ἀναστασις ἡ ἐκ νεκρων, as in Luke xx. 35, and Acts iv. 2, " the resurrection *from* the dead " (d'entre les morts), that is meant, and not the fact of a general resurrection at last, as in Acts. xvii. 32.   The distinction usually made in the New Testament between the resurrection *of* and that *from* the dead, is well worth studying, for the reason given (Rev. xx. 6.)

Reader, unworthy as you *must be*, as one born of fallen parents, would you be *accounted* worthy to obtain *that* world and *the* Resurrection *from* the dead ?   Look to one that was *made* sin for us (himself knowing no sin), " that we might be made the righteousness of God in Him." 2 Cor. v. 21.

INSPIRATION.

THE writers of the Old and New Testaments were employed at different times and on different occasions, in very various tasks.   Such, for instance, were—

1. Writing the words of the Most High, uttered in the audience of others. 2. The mind and intention of God revealed to themselves alone. 3. The words of Satan addressed to God and Christ. 4. The words of wicked men; inspired, as Baalam, or uninspired, as Cain. 5. The words of good men; inspired, as Agabus, or uninspired as Nicodemus. 6. The words of indifferent persons in common conversation. 7. The thoughts of other men; right, as in Luke vii. 39, or wrong, as in Isaiah xi. 13. 8. Their own thoughts; past or *present*, right or wrong, wise or foolish. 9. Prayers of their own, or of others. 10. Events of former, their own, or future days. 11. Quotations from records or decrees, and copies of inscriptions. [Query; anything else?]

Now, the real question is, not "Could the writers do any of these without the Holy Spirit"? but "Are there any of these which He, if He saw fit, could not do, for or with them?"

ADVERSARIA ON THE GREEK TESTAMENT.

1 JOHN V. 16.—A friend lately asked me whether the end of this verse might not be rendered, "I do not say that he should *ask* about it," in the sense of mere questioning, out of curiosity. As far as the mere verb ἐρωταω is concerned, that is certainly its ordinary meaning: and, at the moment, I consented to it. But now, looking at the context, I feel reproved for my want of familiarity with the Greek Testament. The emphasis thrown upon ἐκεινης by its position, *compels* us to take it—"It is not about *that* sin that I am saying he should pray." *This* meaning of ἐρωταω also is supported by John, xiv. 16, xvii. 9—20, and other scriptures.

ROCK OF AGES.

Fissa mei causâ, sæclorum regia Rupes,
In latebris sedes sit mihi fida tuis.

* "*Present*."—John xxi. 25. Perhaps the *sole* instance.

Sit cruor ille tuus, sit aquæ (par nobile!) rivus,
　　Vulnere qui lateris prosiluere tui—
Sint mihi peccati duplex medicamen adempti,
　　Me purgent sceleris crimine vique simul.
Haud-quàquam manuum duri potuere labores
　　Supplendæ legis suppeditare vices.
Si mihi sit studium quod delassare nequires,
　　Perpetuo madeant si mihi rore genæ,
Peccavi! sontemque piacula nulla resolvent,
　　Præter te solum stat mihi nulla salus.
Nil manibus, pretium vitæ, portare paravi,
　　Immorior ligno simpliciterque tuo.
Nil opis in nobis; à te quæro usque favorem,
　　Ad te velandus, vestis egenus, eo.
Fontis ad illustrem fugio turpissimus undam,
　　Emoriar certè, Tu nisi me ipse laves.
Ultima dum dederit suspiria pectus anhelum,
　　Lumina cum Mortis presserit alta quies,
Cum demùm ignotas trepidus ferar hospes in auras,
　　Sederis et solio Tu super ipse tuo,
Fissa mei causâ, sæclorum regia Rupes,
　　In latebris sedes sit mihi fida tuis.

BRITONS.

WE were, in the Roman world, *proverbially* the "uttermost part of the earth," when the Lord used that expression, Acts i. 8, for we were a *little* farther off than our Bretagne neighbours, "Extremi hominum Morini, and were, in fact, designated unceremoniously by the Roman poet, "penitus toto divisos orbe Britannos." The nucleus, so to speak, of whatever measure of true, *i.e.* life-giving, life-forming Christianity, (Galatians ii. 22) now exists in this Gentile Island and

Empire, existed beyond all doubt at a very early period. Dismissing all dubious tradition, we find Martial the Roman Epigrammatist, complimenting Claudia Ruffina, by an assertion which might now be made, wholesale, without conveying any compliment whatever, but *far the other way.* He asks her how it comes to pass that she, though only a simple Cymraes, came to be possessed of all the elegance and attractions of a Roman or Athenian lady. Show me the Italian or Greek now-a-days, who will surpass the Elette of a Denbigh Eisteddfod, as represented by Erddig, Raggat, Pengwern, &c., in 1827 ? But this by the way. The lady whom Martial addresses in the following elegant lines, (O si sic omnia !) was the Claudia to whom the Apostle Paul sends messages of Christian love :—

> Claudia cæruleis cum sit Ruffina Britannis,
>> Edita, cur Latiæ pectora plebis habet ?
> Quale decus formæ ! Romauæ credere matres,
>> Italides possunt, Atthides esse suam !
>>>> Martial Lib. ii. Epig. 54.

This Lady's name is thus Romanized from the British Gwladys Ruffydd (= Griffith); and now, ye Griffiths, which of you can trace up to this truly noble Cymraes? Out with your pedigrees!

And, as the author of our interesting little historical sketch Drych y Prifoesydd well observes, it is not credible that this great lady of Cæsar's household would rest till she had persuaded the Apostle either to go or send to her beloved country, (for true Britons have ever loved their country,) in order to make known *there* the unsearchable riches of Christ, which in the providence of God, through emigration, had become hers. So that, without pressing the evidence for any *individual's* missionary visit to these shores, may we not confidently date the commencement of a British *church*, in the only true sense of that elastic word, from the residence of the Apostle at Rome?

ADVERSARIA ON THE GREEK TESTAMENT.

HEBREWS, ix. 12.—"Should the words in italics, 'for us,' be retained?" They are not necessary; but at least harmless, and perhaps help the meaning. N.B.—The subject of italics is a very important and interesting one. They very inadequately, and *often inconsistently* represent *one* form of difference between the original and the translation; but are, of course, apt to be mistaken for emphatic words. As they are often important to the sense, and the accurate adjustment of them would be extremely difficult, it is to be hoped they will not be rashly interfered with.

1 TIMOTHY, vi. 5.—Should most decidedly be "that godliness is gain;" *i.e.*, that *the* profession of Godliness is *a* way of making money. The article settles this question: it must be with the *subject*, not the predicate.

From a Letter to a Friend.

2 TIMOTHY, i. 10.—But manifested now through the appearing of our saviour Jesus Christ; who-abolished death, and brought-to-light life and immortality through the gospel.

"I think 'through the gospel' applies strictly to *both* propositions so that it might stand *well enough* where you place it" (viz., after "death"). "Surely, where the gospel is *not* received, death is *not* abolished. The *blue ink* marks" (so in M.S., replaced here by italics) "are to be viewed as a separate subject, and are an *attempt* to show the difference between the Greek idiom and the English. In this verse, the attempt seems quite successful; it is not always so easy. It is the only way I ever met with for seeing at one view, the exact *meaning* in English, and the *structure* of the Greek. If you won't try the 'blue ink,' I will decorate for you any verse you will send, very plainly translated in *black* ink. And I think *you* will often find it throws light upon the text, besides the benefit I propose to *myself*, &c. Surely *some* kind hand will do this for me, now and then, at your request." *N.B.—This invitation is now general.*

———

THE following notes on the Verb Substantive " ἐιμι to be," would have appeared sooner if I had found them. I think the subject a *very* important one, capable of affecting many statements of vital consequence, if not the whole of truth as expressed or expressible in language.

A question about *words* is necessarily an idle question, only when it is mistaken for one about *facts;* a mistake which wastes a whole evening in the discussion of a point where there are not, and *could not be,* two opinions! This is a "Logomachy." But a verbal question, taken up advisedly as such, *is* a question of fact, viz.: a fact of language; and may, in its place, be as weighty as any other question whatever. A friend wrote as follows (about December, 1862) :—Referring to the texts Matt. xxvi., 26-28 —"τουτο ἐστι"—Mark, xiv. 22-24, Luke, xxii. 19-20, he asks, "Is the presence of the Greek verb, ' ἐιμι to be,' in a sentence to be understood as if it were *not* there in our idiom, and its absence, as if it *were* there? In the first case, would it read thus: ' This (ἐστι) *represents* my body;' and without ἐστι 'this *is* my body?'"

I replied :—It seems to me hardly *possible*, that a word, when "absent," (*i.e.*, omitted, or understood,) should have a *more* forcible meaning than when present, (*i.e.*, expressed.)

The *very opposite* might be urged, plausibly; but I think not truly, either. *E'στι*, the Latin est, &c., are apt to be omitted when their use, as "Copula," is *evidently* implied. Thus, "Omnia præclara rara," *could* only mean "All illustrious things *are* rare:" and, *therefore*, sunt is dispensed with; as it commonly is, in adages. In all the above texts, even if *ἐστι* were absent from half of them, (as it is actually from *one* only,) it *must*, I believe, be translated "this *is* my body," and the only question *can* be whether the expression is *literally*, or only *figuratively* true, as in "I *am* the door." And that question seems to me to affect the *nouns*, "body," "blood," "door," and not the verb "am," which retains its own proper meaning in either case. "*E'ιμι* to be," has only two uses, viz.: the above use as a "copula," which "asserts something of something," or else as the expression of existence, as *θεος ἐστι* = a God *exists*, or there *is* a God. To say that *ἐστι of itself*, means "represents," seems to me outrageous! But be sure to write again about this. There must be some history connected with your question.

N.B.—I felt sure this idea had been forced upon my worthy correspondent either by men or books; and, accordingly, it turned out that a Greek Testament Lexicon actually gives "represent" as *one* meaning of poor *ἐιμι*! So I afterwards wrote: "The question about *ἐιμι* is, I think, not a question of any dialect, or even of any language, but of language universally. Bagster's little Lexicon, at the end of a Greek Testament here, utterly ignores those supposed meanings. If I knew the author of the one you saw, I would write to him. That verb is kept out oftener than any other, just *because* it must have that one meaning; therefore, the blank is supplied by the mind, with absolute certainty. What *could* "Dux femina facti" mean, but " a woman *was* leader of the exploit?" In English, it is (*idiomatically*) almost always *expressed.* Proverbs, such as, "The more haste (there is), the less speed" (there is), are the only exceptions I can think of. But, how well babies get on without it! "Baby good," "baby tired," &c., are understood by every one; which proves that, even in English, this habit of constantly inserting it, is *merely* idiomatical, and not essential.

I afterwards (*i.e.*, about February 14th, 1848) learnt that, in parables, as Matt. xiii. 37-39; or in symbols, as Rev. iv. 5, and v. 6-8; or quotations, as Matt. xii. 7; this verb is supposed to be used in a peculiar sense, such as to "represent" or "to mean." Now, observe that if this were not, from its very *nature*, purely a question of words; *i.e.*, if it only concerned the *sense* of some detached passages, it might seem idle to enquire whether " I am the door," should be paraphrased 'I [figuratively]-*am* the door'; *i.e.*, I *represent* the door; or ' I am the [figurative]-door' —' I am the [antitype]-door,' or the like; thus transferring the peculiarity from the *verb*, to the following *noun.* But, where the only question before us is about the meaning of the *verb* word ἐιμι, this discussion is *not* an idle one, but simply *to the point.* In safe hands the meaning of individual passages, may sometimes (as above) be not in the least affected by qualifying the *verb* " *is* " or " *am*," (*i.e.*, the "*copula*" in any form,) rather than the *nouns*, (" predicates,") " door," " body," in the propositions '*I am* the door.' 'This *is* my body.' And, of course, nothing is more true than that the *exact meaning* of many other sentences may be preserved sometimes, though you change EVERY NOUN and VERB in those sentences. But, if you once decide that the verb ἐιμι of ITSELF shall not always signify "to *be*," but sometimes " to *mean*," " to *represent*," &c., I think it would introduce such a revolution in language and thought, that no assertion, *divine* or *human,* would have any fixed value. The innumerable instances which *might* be quoted, or framed, to support such a practice (most plausibly, at first sight) will, I believe, *all* turn out to be *conventional abridgements,* where the mind readily supplies the ellipsis, or apprehends the *irony,* without note or comment. An actor may say, " *I am* Hamlet to-night : " when " *Hamlet* " *evidently* means one dressed and speaking as Hamlet: and it is superfluous to look for any strange meaning in the verb " am." The speaker *actually* IS that which any hearer would *naturally* understand by ' *Hamlet,*' as uttered by *him.* And a man in a wheel-barrow may say, " this *is* my coach and six : " when " coach and six " would be at once understood as his jocular term for the one wheeled vehicle, without troubling the *verb* to assume any extraordinary meaning [if it *could,* in that case (?)]. " C'est çà que c'est Toulon," said young Napoleon, with his finger on the map. The General corrected his Geography ! not from misunderstanding the verb " *est,*" but from taking Toulon literally; whilst his " little Corporal" meant *the very spot that commanded Toulon,* and expressed it in one word. " L'Empire c'est la paix," said Napoleon the Third, with the *family conciseness.* Our newspapers rendered it FREELY, " The Empire *means* peace :" rightly enough, *as* a *free* translation. But, if you take the *phrase *to pieces,* and conclude that the French verb " *est* " *of itself, ever* signifies "means," you are, I believe, in serious error. In Matthew, xiii. 37, we have what is called a " convertible proposition." Both σπειρων and υἱος having the article, the sentence might run the *opposite* way, " The Son of man is the sower." In *that* case, " *is* " would not be (by your friend) supposed equivalent to " *meaneth* " or " *representeth,*" but on the contrary

to "*is meant by*," or "*is represented by*." Does it not
strike you as being rather *unlikely*, that the *same verb*
should, *of itself*, with equal facility, adopt either the active
or passive signification of those two verbs? and is it not
more *reasonable* to explain the two propositions, respectively as follows :—The person represented by the sower, or the
(so-called) sower—or the "sower," *really is* the Son of man?
And again: The Son of man *really is* the (above-named)
"sower?"   "More reasonable," I say, because such fillings-
up of ellipses, or expansions of abridgements, are merely such
as you or I would be *obliged* to employ, if required to explain
fully a great proportion of our ordinary conversation.
Whereas, the *other* method confers on the simplest and
most importantly definite of all verbs, the power of assum-
ing, to suit a *good* purpose, [and, therefore, equally to suit
a *bad* one—why not? if once you concede the power,] other
far less definite significations ; giving room to question the
positiveness of *every* such assertion whatever!   The one
method takes no new liberty with language ; but gets out
the truth by a method in *constant* and *unavoidable* use:
the other gets out the *same* truth (nothing *more, or better*),
by an innovation which seems to me replete with *danger*.
If you say, "*what* danger? sure there are *plenty* of words,
with two or more meanings," I answer, there are *more than
enough* already ; and dictionaries needlessly *multiply* the
meanings of words.   Let us not then *add* to the list a word
of all others, perhaps, the *most fixed* in all languages : *the*
vehicle of every assertion : *the* answer of every such question
as "what *is* this?" the *backbone* of *every* other verb,
since "the Lord *reigneth*" resolves itself into "the Lord *is*
reigning," or '*is* King ;' the Root of "Being," "Essence,"
"Entity," &c., &c., the keystone in the arch of language!
Your passage, this *is* my body, can, I allow, be *shortly* dis-

posed of in this way : but at a *fearful expense,* if you fairly
allow all adversaries the liberty of interpreting this same
verb "fast and loose," *ad libitum.* I would say—"this,
though *literally* mere bread, *actually is* my body, *in a certain sense.*" "I *actually am* the vine, the door—the
shepherd, &c., *in a certain sense." What* these several
" senses " *are* the Spirit will teach the humble enquirer.
Nay more ; if the SS. be studied by an *ordinary critic,* with
the same candour as *other* writings, no more difficulty at-
taches to these expressions, than to the figurative language
of Homer, or Virgil, or Cicero, or Dr. Johnson. If you
notice verse *thirty-eight* (Matt. xiii.), syntax would, in
strictness, require each clause to be transferred *backwards ;*
for σπερμα being singular, and ζιζανια *neuter* plural, neither
can *agree* with the verb ἐισι. But, I admit that " attrac-
tion " often supersedes " concord : " and the two *last* clauses
(in verse 39) require, by *rule,* the authorised rendering.

* Note—on taking a phrase to pieces. (Suprā) In
Latin, " *Est mihi*" means " I *have,*" and is the EXACT equivalent of *ego habeo.* But, the separate word '*est*' does not
mean '*have ;*' nor does '*mihi*' mean '*I ;*' they mean and
always *must* mean, " *is* " and " *to me.*" " A book *is to me,*"
is the *common* Latin way of expressing " I *have* a book."
[*Never,* I think, " I have *the* book."] Weigh this fact *well.*

By collecting instances, *consistently* refusing to modify
the *noun* (or predicate), and throwing *all* the burden of explanation on the *verb,* you would have to ascribe so *many*
significations to εἰμι, *besides* to 'represent,' and 'to mean,'
that your friend would be alarmed at the consequences of
his own theory, and glad to confine it to its *old-fashioned*
limits as—1st, the copula ; and 2nd, the verb of *existence.*
1. Θεος ἠν ὁ λογος. 2. ἐστι Θεςς. He appears to consider
this as a question for *Greek* only; but it seems to be for

language generally.　What is true or untrue of "is," will be true or untrue of "ἐστι," and vice versâ.　There *may* be languages where this would not hold good ; but, *as far as I know*, this removes the *reason* he gave you for his opinion, which you copied.

I have written part over again, and made some additions which, I hope, render my meaning *clearer*.　I may ask you again for these ten pages.　Who is the author of the G. T. Lexicon you speak of?　I should be very glad to prevent that rendering of ἐιμι appearing in another edition, and so would the author too.　(It turned out to be Parkhurst. Compare ἐιμι in Scott and Liddell.)

———

ROBERT HALDANE, Esquire.

1 Cor. vii.—The remarks that follow are very often uppermost in my mind, when occupied with Greek Testament questions ; and would, I think, have taken precedence of anything else whatever, but for the grateful recollection that I am entirely indebted for them to the late Robert Haldane, whose name ought to command attention to his few but comprehensive writings, from all those who have time for other religious reading besides their Bibles.　I have, however, since those days (when I got "a read" of them from that *dear old Scot*, John Dove, of Berkeley Square, Bristol), met with many Bible students, who were not only unacquainted with R. H.'s works, but as ignorant as I had previously been myself of those passages which he has rendered so clear.　This alone ought to have removed all objection to figuring in borrowed plumes.　And, in fact, those parts of our knowledge which we can trace directly to a foreign source, are very often quite as *truly* " original " as

other parts which we are perfectly nnconscious of having derived from our fellow-men. Each individual's knowledge is a strange and heterogeneous compound, the constituents of which can no more be referred to their original source than the pebbles in a conglomerate can be traced to the very rock from which they were broken. So that, whilst unacknowledged copying is now and then deservedly shown up, the attempt to be absolutely original, and to have no one to thank, is romantic and impracticable.

It is in connection with the subject of INSPIRATION that the above eminent evangelist took up this chapter in his valuable work on the Evidences of Christianity. And he has so explained it (more by a correct rendering, and calling attention to facts, than by his own comments), as to remove, at once and for ever, from my own mind, what had been to me, in common with many others, *the grand* stumbling block to a simple reception of that all-important doctrine, upon which the whole of God's truth may be said to rest. Unless the " Canon of Scripture" be so assured to us, that we may *now* say of the whole Bible, from Genesis to Revelation, that *all* those holy men of old spake and wrote as they were moved by the Holy Ghost, our minds are liable to be unsettled to any extent on the most vital points, even so as to have, at last, no final appeal either for doctrine or practice. It is therefore a very serious evil, if any portions of the Word of God itself be so misunderstood, as to weaken our confidence in the whole. And, whatever doubts I might have about repeating Mr. Haldane's comment, they would have been entirely removed, by a letter just received from an old Christian friend, in which, after quoting the 6th and 40th verses of this chapter, he asks, " Do these passages imply any doubt as to whether Paul had the mind of the Spirit or not?"

This question is best answered by considering these passages, along with two or three others, which Haldane brings to bear upon the subject so conclusively, that it is to me a matter of regret that such a question should ever have been asked, since the publication of his book many years ago. These passages are, I think (for I gave away the only copy I was possessed of), only the 10th, 12th and 25th of this chapter, and the 37th of the xiv., to which I now invite my correspondent's and my other readers' close and serious attention. First, as to verse 6: Τουτο δε λεγω κατα συγγνωμην, ου κατ᾽ ἐπιταγην would be most simply rendered—"But this I tell you *as* a permission, not *as* a commandment:" which is in evident accordance with the context, for he is neither *absolutely enjoining* marriage nor celibacy, but *allowing* one *or* the other, according to circumstances specified. That the *full* meaning is "as a permission *from God*," seems to me a *perfect matter of course*, even if no other verses were found to corroborate that opinion. But we shall see. In the 10th and 12th verses we find, severally, these two expressions, " Not I, but the Lord," and, " I, not the Lord." In the former case, it was not necessary to give a new commandment by the apostle, because our Lord *had already*, during his personal ministry on earth, decided that a wife must not depart from her husband. In the latter case, when there was *no* previous enactment to refer to, it *was* necessary to make the apostle the vehicle of a *fresh* precept, to meet a case *not* yet provided for, and where Old Testament analogy might naturally have led to the repudiation of unbelieving partners *with their children,* as unclean. See Ezra x. and Neh. xiii. This seems to me the simplest possible acceptation of those two verses, 10 and 12, to the perpetual banishment of a monstrous alternative, viz., that the Apostle Paul should be giving the Corinthians the mind of God and his own notions *by turns*, after having "obtained mercy of the Lord to be faithful," in communicating *his* blessed will on most weighty questions! It is now needless to comment, in verse 25, on the words, "I have no commandment of the Lord;" as it is a simple historical fact, that the ministry of Jesus had not provided for the case in point; but γνωμην διδωμι simply means, "I give judgment." If, however, the words *had* been την ἐμην γνωμην, as in verse 40, (*i.e., my* judgment) there would be nothing more perplexing in that than the expression, "*my* gospel," which, I suppose, never misled any one, any more than the words, "I speak not by commandment," in 2 Cor. viii. 8 ; which though identical, both in Greek and English, with the 6th verse of our chapter, was probably never supposed to mean, "not by God's commandment," but "not *as* a commandment," or "not *by way* of commandment," *i.e.,* only by way of *exhortation.* On the other hand, in 1 Tim. i. 1, the very same words, κατ' ἐπιταγην, with the context, Θεου σωτηρος, &c., obviously do mean, "by the commandment of God," &c. These distinctions I believe will commend themselves to the sober judgment of every scholar.

As to verse 40, it is only necessary to say that the verb δοκω, translated "I think," is the very same which in Luke xvii. 9 is rendered, "I *trow* not," where no uncertainty is implied, but quite the contrary ; and finally, that *in this very epistle*, where "την ἐμην γνωμην," &c., have been supposed to throw some doubt upon the inspiration of the writer, he himself says, in the most positive terms, "If any man think himself to be a prophet or spiritual, let him acknowledge that the things that *I* write unto *you*, are *the commandments of the Lord.*"—Chap. xiv. 37. Cadit quæstio—May these helps from Robert Haldane be blessed to

others as they have been to me ; and to God be the praise.
I can now refer to his work, in 2 vols. 8vo, 1834, vol. I.,
chap. 5, pages, 169-172. Those who reject his explanation,
have the alternative of believing that the Apostle—

1. Laid down rules for their guidance, *knowing* that he
had God's permission, but yet *no express commandment* to
do so (v. 6.) :

2. That he afterwards gives the Lord's mind and his
own mind *by turns* (verses 10, 12, 25), and ventures *his own,*
where he has, in a very difficult question, to set aside Old
Testament precedents (12, 13); concluding, " *and so I ordain in all the churches* " (v. 17):

3. That he could take these wanton liberties, instead of
waiting for the Lord's directions, and yet assert that he is
" one that hath obtained mercy of the Lord *to be faithful*:"

4. That he means by verse 40, that he is *not sure,* in
that particular instance, whether it is the *Lord's* mind or
his own that he his delivering :

5. That, after *all* this, he insists upon an acknowledg-
ment (xiv. 37), that the things he writes to these very Corinthians are the commandments of the Lord.

INSPIRATION.

A FRIEND once asked me whether I did not think the
literary and scientific portion of society had a claim upon
serious exponents of the Word of God, for a clear line of
demarcation between the doctrinal statements of holy writ,
and matters therein of a merely historical or scientific
nature. I promised to consider the question (as we were
then hurried), only adding, that whatever else God thought
fit to tell us *besides* the way of salvation, he told us *from
himself,* and therefore *truly.*

IN ANSWER TO A QUESTION FROM A FRIEND.

" 1 PETER, iv. 11.—I prefer '*the* oracles,' as it stands, to your omission of the article.   Observe that λογια θεου and *Ta* λογια του θεου *may* mean *exactly* the same thing, and also that, in English, 'God's oracles' without any article, has the *full* force of '*the* oracles of God.'   Had this passage, however, been rendered 'oracles of God,' one could not have found fault.   Too much stress has been laid on the presence or absence of the article ; (especially in Taylor's 'Emphatic Testament;' a well-meant and interesting book.)   And no *rules* will ever teach any one to appreciate such points."

" HEBREWS, vi. 1.—The masculine word βαπτισμος *never*, I believe, means the ordinance of Baptism ; merely ' washings,' such as of cups, &c."

TWO PARAGRAPHS PLEADING FOR " LEVIORA " IN
O. P.'S REMAINS.

" IT is an utterly unwarranted view that ascribes the serious wholly to God, and the humorous wholly to the devil : human nature does possess this two-fold side ; and both have been given it by God."   From " Better days for working people," quoted in *British Messenger*, for August, 1863 ; title, HOUSEHOLD SUNSHINE.

ON the most deliberate reflection, I retain the view taken of merriment in 1863, believing it to be quite separable from sinful love of the world, and to be the lawful and special privilege of little children, young men, or fathers, such as St. John addresses in his 1st. Epistle, i. 12-15, who ought therefore to *insist* on it, within due bounds, as necessary to the mental and physical health which they need for their Master's service.

A Reception at Syracuse ; about b.c. 240.

"Are you there Archie?"—*Binnie McLaren.*

You never mean to say you came, that figure, through the
   street?   [*Stark naked, shouting "Heureka, Heureka."*]
And market-day! well, country folk at last *have* had a treat.
"You've *found* it!" well, what *have* you found? no earthly
   good, I guess;
You're always "finding" something—could you not find
   time to dress?
Perhaps you didn't *find* it cold, but—how could you for
   shame?
Then some would think you *had* no clothes, and *I* should
   get the blame!   [*See "Miseries of Human Life.'*]
Rather than make your Missiz out a good-for-nothing swab,
(And you in such a hurry too) you *might* have called a cab.
"Come from the bath"—all very well, but why without
   your clothes?   [*Nods knowingly.*]
Those wide-awake Lopodytæ have boned 'em, I suppose.
On second thoughts I fancy though,—nay, more, I have
   no doubt,   [*Shakes her head gravely.*]
You've pawned 'em for a drop o' drink; they're all gone up
   the spout!
I hear—the old apology,—"absence of mind," foorsoth!
Absence of all propriety would come far nearer truth.
Saving your *presence*, absent Sir, it's really past excuse,
To go like that and make yourself the talk of Syracuse.
Now, really, Archimedes, I can't tell you how I'm vexed;
A pretty crotchet this indeed—pray what will be the next?
Well, for the sake of argument, granting "you *are* a tough
   one,"
Yet, for appearance sake I think you *never* have enough on.
"It suits your slender means," you say, "to dress a little
   coolish!"

I don't call that economy, but " penny wise pound foolish."
When tired of this buff jerkin that you're now accoutred in,
I dare say by-and-by you'll try to go without a skin !
Such pranks are, Archimedes, more than I *can* endure ;
To *live* with a Philosopher is not a sinecure.
That rainy day I had to shout as loud as I could bellow,
" You've taken baby's parasol instead of your umbrella ! "
You never seem to me to know what 'tis you have to do ;
And who do you suppose is to be trotting after *you !*
" You never thought of it ! " that is, it wasn't *worth* a
    thought :
" You never thought of it," indeed ! then, I maintain, you
    ought.
What ever did you dream about, that made you take to
    flight ?
" *Specific* gravity," indeed ! that upsets *mine* outright.
" An accident," I hear you say ; " an *accident*," indeed !
If so, then " accidental death " for killing you I'll plead.
¶ For killing *me ?* μαρτυρομαι ! (you, slaves, must all have
    heard her,)
That very word would justify a charge of wilful murder.
¶ Now, Archimedes, really I'm surprised at your assurance ;
That you should think of answ'ring so, is simply past en-
    durance ! [*Stamps and screams.*]
And now I swear by all the gods and goddesses infernal,
Since you've exposed yourself in town, I'll do so in the
    Journal.
You care for no one class of men, mob, demus, nor the
    great,
And so, (for *something* must be done) I'll try the Fourth
    Estate.
I'll tell the story as it is, and not suppress one particle,
You, in the *Syracusan Times*, shall be the leading article.

In *Daily News* and *Telegraph* the reading world shall
  spy all ;
And then to make the thing complete, I'll post you in
  the DIAL ! ! !
You've often asked a *stand*ing place—the wisest word you
  spoke !
To verify your δος που στω, you'll be a standing joke.
You'll figure to the end of time as " He that bawled εὑρηκα,"
A laughing-stock to school boys in their Analecta Græca.

PHILOLOGY FOR THE MILLION.

SEVEN OAKS AND NINE ELMS.—DEDICATED TO DEAN TRENCH.

I've often thought of those 2 names ; think of them with
  me, please:
Those trees, to a reflecting mind, are 16 pleasantries.

THAMES BOATMAN LOQUITUR.

Sevenhoaks is—no—7 hoaks *are*—no, Sevenhoaks *is* down
  in Kent ;
Yes, *hoax* is always singular, and that's the hoax they
  meant.
Nine Helms are—no—9 Helms *is*—no Nine Helms *are* by
  Vauxhall ;
So put your *helms* a-starboard, lads, or else a-port, that's
  all.
But, "why say 7?" or "why say 9?" if you should still de-
  mand,
There's many things in figures as we *cannot* understand.
They talk of our 4 fathers, yet *one* served for me and you :
Three pair can play a game at *fives*, and *single*-stick needs
  two !

EN REVANCHE.

A SLIP of a girl fell into the water last month, at Birken-head, and was saved by her crinoline! What made Virgil say, "*inutile* ferrum Cingitur?" N.B.—Some say *she* had no drowning mark upon her; and I much incline thereto.

TRANSLATE, Integer vitæ, the whole of life; and sceleris purus, a poor (stick) of celery.—*Hor. Od.*

If jus pueri means Broth of a boy, (and what else *can* it mean?) how shall we adequately render "Jus *trium* liberorum?"

"Nimium ne crede colori!" = Take care of the paint!

"Seniores priores," said fingers to spoons.

A PROVINCIAL journal informs us, that a certain Roman Catholic priest, who has censured the rich and poor with equal severity, has been "tattooed," and banished from polite society for his faithfulness. We would not be *in his skin!* "In cute curandâ *plùs æquo* operata juventus," would be hardly fair, if applied, after this severe retribution, to *that* youth. Nay, rather, "Ire domum hunc et cuticulam curare *jubeto.*"

"CAWS WEBI BOBI; SAIS WEDI GROGI."

I LEARNT this adage, motto, device, or whatever it may be called, from my estimable friend, Dean Conybeare, whose pronunciation of the two main words, bôbi and grôgi, greatly enhanced the intrinsic richness of the aphorism. Can any reader (why not Old Devinez?) assist me in elucidating its purport? By internal evidence, it betrays a Silurian origin; for, assuredly, "Caws webi bobi," in *North* Wales, would not mean *toasted* but *baked* cheese. I have two theories respecting it—1st, " Cheese toasted and an Englishman hanged," may have been designed to teach the proper destiny of those two respectively artificial and natural productions; if so, it would stand in Latin—Ut caseus ad torrendum, ita Saxo ad pendendum natus est. That this expresses A GREAT FACT few of *my* countrymen will doubt for a moment. There is, however, a deeper meaning of which the words are susceptible; and I rather think our Southern neighbours, an acute and pugnacious race, deserve the credit of *it*, rather than of the commonplace sentiment above proposed. " Wedi bobi" and " wedi grogi" are evidently *correlative* terms; and they are both capable of a *culinary* acception: the latter being actually, in any part of Wales, used as an equivalent to the English particle " hung," as applied to beef. In this point of view, the phrase would be a terrific and ostentatious war-cry, implying that the fierce aborigines would as soon devour a rasher of their invaders (properly cured) as a dish of Welsh Rabbit! Not that our brave ancestors ever *were* cannibals, any more than the Crusaders, who *pretended* to be so in order to strike terror into the Saracens. But it would serve the purpose of intimidation on the grand scale, to inform the intruder in those rude ages, not that you would *give* his flesh to the fowls of the air (thank you), but *keep* it for your own family use* about Christmas. And it may well be supposed to have a peculiar effect on the nervous system of JEAN ROSBIF'S progenitor to learn, through an interpreter, that the islander whose home he had disturbed could not only *beat* but also *eat* him with his own weapons; and, after fighting, pro aris et focis, would cook the slain, at his leisure, before the very hearth which they had sought to

* See " The Grewsome Caryl," by Hogg.—*Edin. Rev.*

desecrate when living. But query whether Caws webi bobi, Sais wedi grogi, may not have involved a *still more* recondite signification? Meanwhile, an excellent friend of mine has "rejoiced the cockles of my heart" by suggesting (according to Œdipus' hearty $\dot{\epsilon}\iota$ $\kappa\alpha\iota$ $\tau\rho\iota\tau'$ $\dot{\epsilon}\sigma\tau\iota$—) a *third* interpretation, which I confidently offer to the acceptance of every genuine GWLADGARWR. It is this:—The hanging of a Sais being evidently a highly meritorious action, Taffy may be supposed to have fairly " earned his dinner" thereby, and to sit down to his Caws wedi bobi with all the better conscience and appetite, when he was able to report Sais (neu ddau?) wedi grogi! Thus he. I don't give his name, lest his Bishop should not admire the idea *quite* so much as I do. $\pi\lambda\epsilon\iota$ $\delta\epsilon$ $\dot{\epsilon}\tau\iota!$ quoth Poseidon, in Lucian, Dial. vi. Or, 4thly, was it simply an announcement of 1st and 2nd course in the Bill of Fare of a Welsh ordinary, in the good old times?

> This is, perhaps, the truer view,
> NOTES AND QUERIES, what say *you?*

ENIGMAS.

1. See Virgil hys Eneis Book y^e fyrste and line 113 and you shall fynde—
  " Unam, quæ Lycios fidumque vehebat Orontem."
and severalle dayntie lines followynge. Havynge redde the same, well and *warily*, tell me, Gentle Reder, whether (in your judgment) ye sayde Orontes was hedde over ye Lycians solely and exclusively, or over other beside them?

2. What is the shortest Greek translation of—
(*a*) A compact body of cavalry (β) To dine off short commons.

3. Illustrate, from a Roman poet, the weariness of a sedentary life.

4. Give an instance of a standing joke from Plautus.

5. What, in Virgil, is the opposite to Arma virumque?

6. How may δειπνειν be resolved into elements essential to the act denoted by that verb?

7. What Philosopher deserved to be roasted alive?

8. What *sort* of a horse did Minerva give Bellerophon?

9. What is the most *correct* French for " Mr. and Mrs. Okell?"

10. What sort of verses suit the realms of Pluto?

11. What Latin phrase describes *in two words*, the happy accouchement at Frogmore?

MOTTOES SUGGESTED.

For the Prince of Wales, *as such*, " Jus et Lēx," *i.e.*, Broth and Leeks ; by a Hendiadys for " Leek Broth," as " Pateris libamus et auro." *h.e.*, pateris aureis.   Virg.

For the Posse Comitatus, after Bristol Riots—"Possunt, quia posse videntur."

For a Tobacconist—" Quis non te potiùs, Bacche?"—*Hor.*

For John Parry, the singer—" Parræ recinentis omen."— *Ibid.*

For a Lightcake Shop—" Leviora."

For that to'ther Lightcake Shop—" Graviora."

For the same—" Levius fit, patientiâ, *Quid-quid* corrigere est nefas."   So, *chaw* away, my hearties ; they'll mend *in time*.

For a 3rd Lightcake Shop—" Et visco, et Phrygiæ servat pice lentius Idæ!"—*Virg. Geo.* IV.

For a 4th *Lightcake* Shop—" Nil vidi minùs!"

For a Maresnester—"Sic vos non vobis nidificatis, *equæ.*

For a Juvenile Tea-party—" Parúm comis sine *te* Juventus."—*Hor. Odes.* 1, 30.

For a Barometer-maker, the next line—" Mercuriusque."

For Counsellor Temple—Subaudi templum.—*Eton Gram.*

For a Shaker—" Denique teipsum concute."—*Hor.*

For an Undertaker—Vive la Mort.

For Longfellow's Blacksmith—" Ab ipso Ducit opes animumque ferro."—*Hor.*

For a well-dressed Female of 1863—Inutile *ferrum* cingitur."—*Virg.*

For Mr. Hincks—" Hinc atque hinc."—*Virg.*

To one who gets a living by billsticking—" Pasco, pavi, PASTUM."—*Hoole's Terminations.*

For a Beer Shop—"Potus ex hordeo, in quandam similitudinen vini corruptus."—*Tacitus* his *Germany.* For a Protegé of the Humane Society—" Nuper me *in flumine* vidi. For O. P.'s Remains—' Magnas inter OPES in OP's. —*Hor.*

DUOGLOT DISTICHS.

" Canusini more bilinguis !"—*Hor.*

Qui sine fine solet totis tussire diebus,
    Quicquid agant medici, codliveroilus homo est.
Ne Champagna bibas, qui curas ire decenter, .
    Qui Champagna bibit, kickupadustus homo est.
Si forte auctumno citò vis mandata referri,
    Ne mittas Jackum, blackberryosus homo est.
Sive opus est puero, certus qui nuntius ibit,
    Ne credas Billo, pen-yn-y-gwyntus homo est.
Per fas atque nefas siquando rem fieri vis,
    Convenias Thomam, gothewholehoggus homo est.
Rursùs, amice, ratas si spes cupis esse repente,

Ah ! fuge Slowcoachum, stickinthemudus homo est.
Impavido si forte opus est ad bella sodali,
    Ne Quakerum quæras, allofadither homo est.
Vin' socium reperire, latus qui claudat honestè ?
    Evites Irum, worseforthewearus homo est.

BAD LATIN CORRECTED.

By an Enraged Humanity Professor (Not of St. Andrew's.)

This *Bi*centenary, o' whilk ye talk,
Suggests By-ends, By-path, By-views, By-walk.
Hoot ! "gie the Diel his *due*," mon, for the nonce,
An ca' it *Du*centenary at once !

TITLES OF BOOKS.

CHEW MAGNA *versus* BOLT-ON-LE-MOORS;

*A Treatise on the Duty and Privilege of Mastication; addressed to
Hungry Sportsmen.*

Profundior, or Deeper and deeper still ; a Poem by Shortfellow.

Samos ; a treatise on Equine Identity ; by a Veterinary Detective.

Ducks ego vester eram : Reminiscences of Wild-fowl Shooting ; by $T\eta\lambda$-av-$\gamma\eta\varsigma$, = Teal *or* Geese.

A Dying Duet : composed expressly for the Swan with two necks, by a Writer to the Cygnet ; with a Solo for "The Old Swan ;" by Dolichodeirus.

Cloudy Memories ; by a Graduate of Nephelococcygia.

A Tale of a Pail ; by a Milkmaid.

Drink to me only with thine *eye*.   A song to Polyphemus, in the opera Acis and Galatea (*see Spectator*).

ANSWERS TO ENIGMAS.

1. It appeareth from line 116 of the said Eneis, that poor Orontes, hedde over yᵉ Lycians, was no whit less *hedde over heelis.*

2. (a) στιφος = stiff oss. (β) ὀλιγου δειν. How beautifully concise!

3. Sedet, æternùmque sedebit Infelix Theseus. Æneid. vi.

4. Hos quos videtis stare Captivos duos
Illi qui adstant, hi stant ambo, non sedent.

Capt. Prologue.

5. " *No* men, et arma."

6. δει πνειν : since breathing time is essential to a feast. See Paley on the Epiglottis, Nat. Theol.

7. The great Zo-roaster himself, richly.

8. " Oss homini *sublime* dedit.   (*See* Pegasus.)

9. Monsieur *Au*quel et Madame *A*laquelle.

10. " Acrostics," licet respondere tutò (sc. Across Styx).

11. " Facilè Princeps;" which also designates the Royal Lady herself, by all accounts.

FINIS.

[TURN OVER.

MORE LAST WORDS.

SEE p. 115, and observe that *every* body " translates "
R. sceleratus, Celery-leaved Ranunculus! Ask C. C. B.

But now, *seriously,* translate Lucretius, vi. 1230:
" When each saw himself (so) entangled in the disease, that
he *was* (virtually) doomed to death,"—he took it as a
notice to quit, and gave up all hope.

And next, still *more* seriously, (because fortified by the
context, "ita "—"ad arma"—&c.) translate Livy viii. 37, 6:
" *Ita* ex somno, &c." " *So* startled the lieges, that the
capitol, citadel, walls, and gates *were* (actually, ' in no
time ') full of armed men "—i.e., each at his post, " omnibus locis." N.B.—" Fuerint " is just the AORIST—Sub- or
rather *Con*-junctive; *a tense too often overlooked,* my
young friends.

Once more; *try* Virgil, Æneid xi. 268 (an open question, if ever there was one) as follows: " The adulterer
settled-under conquered Asia;" i.e., after Asia was conquered, that base element [in the Eastern Question of the
day] remained behind; as the name stuck, "subsedit," in the
helmet, Æn. v. 498. He constituted την τρυγα, the *dregs* of
that bitter cup. The verb subsidere occurs with " limus,
ut *fœx,*" Lucr. v. 498; with " *fœces* in fundis vasorum,"
Col. 12, 52, 4; with " Bright's disease," in Pl. 28, 6, 19;—
only, *not transitive.* Well, you can't have *every* thing, so—
O vos VALETE !

FINISSIMUS.

Preparing for the Press,

"MARY'S EUCLID,"

Re-printed, with Diagrams, from "Old Price's Remains."

ANDREW & DAVID RUSSELL, PRINTERS,

MOORFIELDS, LIVERPOOL.

www.ingramcontent.com/pod-product-compliance
Lightning Source LLC
Chambersburg PA
CBHW031121020726
47495CB00007B/2302